(more on next page)

(continued from front page)

" I just wanted to thank you for helping me get a great score
on the AP U.S. History exam... Thank you for making great test preps! "
Student, Los Angeles, CA

" Your *Fundamentals of Engineering Exam* book was the absolute best
preparation I could have had for the exam, and it is one of the major
reasons I did so well and passed the FE on my first try. "
Student, Sweetwater, TN

" I used your book to prepare for the test and found that the advice and the
sample tests were highly relevant... Without using any other material, I earned
very high scores and will be going to the graduate school of my choice. "
Student, New Orleans, LA

" What I found in your book was a wealth of information sufficient to shore up
my basic skills in math and verbal... The section on analytical ability was
excellent. The practice tests were challenging and the answer explanations most
helpful. It certainly is the *Best Test Prep for the GRE!* "
Student, Pullman, WA

" I really appreciate the help from your excellent book. Please keep up
the great work. "
Student, Albuquerque, NM

" I am writing to thank you for your test preparation... your book helped me
immeasurably and I have nothing but praise for your *GRE* preparation."
Student, Benton Harbor, MI

THE BEST TEST PREPARATION FOR THE

CLEP

Principles of Microeconomics

With REA's TEST*ware*® on CD-ROM

Richard Sattora, M.S.
Recipient of the Blue Ribbon Teacher of Economics Award
from the Federal Reserve Bank of Dallas

Research & Education Association
Visit our website at:
www.rea.com

Research & Education Association
61 Ethel Road West
Piscataway, New Jersey 08854
E-mail: info@rea.com

The Best Test Preparation for the
CLEP PRINCIPLES OF MICROECONOMICS EXAM
With TEST*ware*® on CD-ROM

Printed in the United States of America

Library of Congress Control Number 2007929868

ISBN-13: 978-0-7386-0312-4
ISBN-10: 0-7386-0312-0

Windows® is a registered trademark of Microsoft Corporation.

REA® and TEST*ware*® are registered trademarks of
Research & Education Association, Inc.

About the Author

Richard Sattora is an AP Economics teacher at Excelsior Award-winning Pittsford Mendon High School, Pittsford, N.Y., where he has taught for 30 years. The caliber of his work has brought Mr. Sattora recognition from *Who's Who Among America's Teachers* and the Federal Reserve Bank of Dallas, where he was designated a "Blue Ribbon Teacher of Economics."

In 2005, under Mr. Sattora's direction, Pittsford Mendon High School's Federal Reserve Challenge Team won the Fed Challenge national championship. This prestigious national economics competition is sponsored by the Board of Governors of the Federal Reserve System and promotes a greater understanding of economics among students. Recently, Mr. Sattora designed an Economic Education Institute blueprint for the Federal Reserve Bank of New York. A graduate of Canisius College, he holds an M.S. degree from Nazareth College.

Mr. Sattora's varied background in economics gives him a balanced perspective on the subject. He has worked for Eastman Kodak Co. and been involved in many entrepreneurial activities in the real estate, restaurant, and landscaping fields. He is a member of the Rochester Area Council of Social Studies and the Association of Private Enterprise Educators.

Author Acknowledgments

I extend special thanks to my wife, Jeanette, and my sons, Jeffrey and Christopher, without whose patience and support this work could not have been completed. I would also like to acknowledge my parents, Howard and Betty, for the special role they played in all of my accomplishments. I am grateful to the former and current staff of the Federal Reserve Bank of Dallas, especially Wayne Hast, whose generosity and support for high school economics teachers allowed me to attend my first APEE conference that began this journey. I also thank other members of the Federal Reserve Bank of Dallas including former President Bob McTeer, Chief Economist C. Michael Cox, and economist Bob Formiani whose presentations and writings continue to educate and inspire me. Finally, I would like to thank the staff of the Federal Reserve Branch Bank of Buffalo, economist Richard Dietz, Kausar Hamdani, and Diana Bley for their support of my Federal Reserve Challenge Team.

About Research & Education Association

Founded in 1959, Research & Education Association (REA) is dedicated to publishing the finest and most effective educational materials—including software, study guides, and test preps—for students in middle school, high school, college, graduate school, and beyond.

REA's test preparation series includes books and software for all academic levels in almost all disciplines. REA publishes test preps for students who have not yet entered high school, as well as high school students preparing to enter college. Students from countries around the world seeking to attend college in the United States will find the assistance they need in REA's publications. For college students seeking advanced degrees, REA publishes test preps for many major graduate school admission examinations in a wide variety of disciplines, including engineering, law, and medicine. Students at every level, in every field, with every ambition can find what they are looking for among REA's publications.

REA's series presents tests that accurately depict the official exams in both degree of difficulty and types of questions. REA's practice tests are always based upon the most recently administered exams, and include every type of question that can be expected on the actual exams.

Today REA's wide-ranging catalog is a leading resource for teachers, students, and professionals.

We invite you to visit us at *www.rea.com* to find out how "REA is making the world smarter."

Acknowledgments

In addition to our author, we would like to thank Larry B. Kling, Vice President, Editorial, for his overall direction; Pam Weston, Vice President, Publishing, for setting the quality standards for production integrity and managing the publication to completion; John Cording, Vice President, Technology, for coordinating the design, development, and testing of REA's TEST*ware*® software; Diane Goldschmidt, Senior Editor, for editorial contributions and project management; Alice Leonard, Senior Editor, Michael Reynolds, Senior Editor, and Molly Solanki, Associate Editor, for editorial contributions; Heena Patel and Amy Jamison, Technology Project Managers, for their design contributions and software testing efforts; Christine Saul, Senior Graphic Designer, for designing our cover; Jeff LoBalbo, Senior Graphic Designer, for coordinating pre-press electronic file mapping; and Kathy Caratozzolo of Caragraphics for typesetting this edition.

CONTENTS

CLEP PRINCIPLES OF MICROECONOMICS
Independent Study Schedule

The following study schedule allows for thorough preparation for the CLEP Principles of Microeconomics exam. Although it is designed for four weeks, it can be reduced to a two-week course by collapsing each two-week period into one. Be sure to set aside enough time—at least two hours each day—to study. But no matter which study schedule works best for you, the more time you spend studying, the more prepared and relaxed you will feel on the day of the exam.

Week	Activity
1	Read and study the Introduction section of this book, which will introduce you to the CLEP Principles of Microeconomics exam. Then take Practice Test 1 on CD-ROM to determine your strengths and weaknesses. Assess your results by using our raw score conversion table. You can then determine the areas in which you need to strengthen your skills.
2 & 3	Carefully read and study the Basic Economics Course Review and CLEP Microeconomics Course Review included in this book.
4	Take Practice Test 2 on CD-ROM and carefully review the explanations for all incorrect answers. If there are any types of questions or particular subjects that seem difficult to you, review those subjects by again studying the appropriate sections of the review material in this book.

Note: If you care to, and time allows, retake Practice Tests 1 and 2 printed in this book. This will help strengthen the areas in which your performance may still be lagging and build your overall confidence.

INSTALLING REA's TEST*ware*®

SYSTEM REQUIREMENTS

Pentium 75 MHz (300 MHz recommended) or a higher or compatible processor; Microsoft Windows 98 or later; 64 MB Available RAM; Internet Explorer 5.5 or higher

INSTALLATION

1. Insert the CLEP Principles of Microeconomics TEST*ware*® CD-ROM into the CD-ROM drive.
2. If the installation doesn't begin automatically, from the Start Menu choose the RUN command. When the RUN dialog box appears, type d:\setup (where *d* is the letter of your CD-ROM drive) at the prompt and click OK.
3. The installation process will begin. A dialog box proposing the directory "Program Files\REA\CLEPMicroeconomics" will appear. If the name and location are suitable, click OK. If you wish to specify a different name or location, type it in and click OK.
4. Start the CLEP Principles of Microeconomics TEST*ware*® application by double-clicking on the icon.

REA's CLEP Principles of Microeconomics TEST*ware*® is **EASY** to **LEARN AND USE**. To achieve maximum benefits, we recommend that you take a few minutes to go through the on-screen tutorial on your computer.

SSD ACCOMMODATIONS FOR STUDENTS WITH DISABILITIES

Many students qualify for extra time to take the CLEP Principles of Microeconomics exam, and our TEST*ware*® can be adapted to accommodate your time extension. This allows you to practice under the same extended-time accommodations that you will receive on the actual test day. To customize your TEST*ware*® to suit the most common extensions, visit our website at *www.rea.com/ssd.*

TECHNICAL SUPPORT

REA's TEST*ware*® is backed by customer and technical support. For questions about **installation or operation of your software**, contact us at:

> **Research & Education Association**
> **Phone: (732) 819-8880 (9 a.m. to 5 p.m. ET, Monday–Friday)**
> **Fax: (732) 819-8808**
> **Website: www.rea.com**
> **E-mail: info@rea.com**

Note to Windows XP Users: In order for the TEST*ware*® to function properly, please install and run the application under the same computer administrator-level user account. Installing the TEST*ware*® as one user and running it as another could cause file-access path conflicts.

▼
INTRODUCTION

Introduction

PASSING THE CLEP PRINCIPLES OF MICROECONOMICS EXAM

ABOUT THIS BOOK AND TEST*ware*®

This book provides you with complete preparation for the CLEP Principles of Microeconomics exam. Inside you will find a targeted review of the subject matter, as well as tips and strategies for test taking. We also give you two practice tests, featuring content and formatting based on the official CLEP Principles of Microeconomics exam. Our practice tests contain every type of question that you can expect to encounter on the actual exam. Following each practice test you will find an answer key with detailed explanations designed to help you more completely understand the test material.

The practice exams in this book and software package are included in two formats: in printed format in this book, and in TEST*ware*® format on the enclosed CD. **We strongly recommend that you begin your preparation with the TEST*ware*® practice exams.** The software provides the added benefits of instant scoring and enforced time conditions.

ABOUT THE EXAM

Who takes CLEP exams and what are they used for?

CLEP (College-Level Examination Program) examinations are typically taken by people who have acquired knowledge outside the classroom and wish to bypass certain college courses and earn college credit. The CLEP is designed to reward students for learning—no matter where or how that knowledge was acquired. The CLEP is the most widely accepted credit-by-examination program in the country, with more than 2,900 colleges and universities granting credit for satisfactory scores on CLEP exams.

Although most CLEP examinees are adults returning to college, many graduating high school seniors, enrolled college students, military personnel, and international students also take the exams to earn college credit or to demonstrate their ability to perform at the college level. There are no prerequisites, such as age or educational status, for taking CLEP examinations. However, because policies on granting credits vary among colleges, you should contact the particular institution from which you wish to receive CLEP credit.

There are two categories of CLEP examinations:

1. **CLEP General Examinations**, which are five separate tests that cover material usually taken as requirements during the first two years of college. CLEP General Examinations are available for English Composition (with or without essay), Humanities, Mathematics, Natural Sciences, and Social Sciences and History.

2. **CLEP Subject Examinations** include material usually covered in an undergraduate course with a similar title. For a complete list of the subject examinations offered, visit the College Board website.

Who administers the exam?

The CLEP tests are developed by the College Board, administered by Educational Testing Service (ETS), and involve the assistance of educators throughout the United States. The test development process is designed and implemented to ensure that the content and difficulty level of the test are appropriate.

When and where is the exam given?

CLEP exams are administered each month throughout the year at more than 1,300 test centers in the United States and can be arranged for candidates abroad on request. To find the test center nearest you and to register for the exam, you should obtain a copy of the free booklets CLEP Colleges and CLEP Information for Candidates and Registration Form. They are available at most colleges where CLEP credit is granted, or by contacting:

CLEP Services
P.O. Box 6600
Princeton, NJ 08541-6600
Phone: (800) 257-9558 (8 a.m. to 6 p.m. ET)
Fax: (609) 771-7088
Website: *www.collegeboard.com/clep*

CLEP Options for Military Personnel and Veterans

CLEP exams are available free of charge to eligible military personnel and eligible civilian employees. All the CLEP exams are available at test centers on college campuses and military bases. In addition, the College Board has developed a paper-based version of 14 high-volume/high-pass-rate CLEP tests for DANTES Test Centers. Contact the Educational Services Officer or Navy College Education Specialist for more information. Visit the College Board website for details about CLEP opportunities for military personnel.

Eligible U.S. veterans can claim reimbursement for CLEP exams and administration fees pursuant to provisions of the Veterans Benefits Improvement Act of 2004. For details on eligibility and submitting a claim for reimbursement, visit the U.S. Department of Veterans Affairs website at *www.gibill.va.gov/pamphlets/testing.htm*.

SSD Accommodations for Students with Disabilities

Many students qualify for extra time to take the CLEP Principles of Microeconomics exam, but you must make these arrangements in advance. For information, contact:

College Board Services for Students with Disabilities
P.O. Box 6226
Princeton, NJ 08541-6226
Phone: (609) 771-7137 (Monday through Friday, 8 a.m. to 6 p.m. ET)
TTY: (609) 882-4118
Fax: (609) 771-7944
E-mail: ssd@info.collegeboard.org

Our TEST*ware*® can be adapted to accommodate your time extension. This allows you to practice under the same extended-time accommodations that you will receive on the actual test day. To customize your TEST*ware*® to suit the most common extensions, visit our website at *www.rea.com/ssd*.

HOW TO USE THIS BOOK

What do I study first?

Read over the course review and the suggestions for test-taking, take the first practice test to determine your area(s) of weakness, and then go back and focus your study on those specific problems. Studying the reviews thoroughly will reinforce the basic skills you will need to do well on the exam. Make sure to take the practice tests to become familiar with the format and procedures involved with taking the actual exam.

To best utilize your study time, follow our Independent Study Schedule, which you'll find in the front of this book. The schedule is based on a four-week program, but can be condensed to two weeks if necessary by collapsing each two-week period into one.

When should I start studying?

It is never too early to start studying for the CLEP Principles of Microeconomics exam. The earlier you begin, the more time you will have to sharpen your skills. Do not procrastinate! Cramming is not an effective way to study, since it does not allow you the time needed to learn the test material. The sooner you learn the format of the exam, the more time you will have to familiarize yourself with it.

FORMAT AND CONTENT OF THE EXAM

The CLEP Principles of Microeconomics exam covers the material one would find in a college-level introductory microeconomics class. The exam requires the test-taker to analyze and evaluate economic decisions, demonstrate an understanding of how free markets work, and understand how individual consumers and firms make economic decisions.

The exam consists of 80 multiple-choice questions, each with five possible answer choices, to be answered in 90 minutes.

The approximate breakdown of topics is as follows:

8–12%	Basic economic concepts
60–70%	The nature and function of the product market
10–15%	Factor Market
4–6%	Market failures and the role of government

ABOUT OUR COURSE REVIEW

The review in this book provides you with a complete background of all the important basic economic concepts and microeconomic principles and theories relevant to the exam. It will help reinforce the facts you have already learned while better shaping your understanding of the discipline as a whole. By using the review in conjunction with the practice tests, you should be well prepared to take the CLEP Principles of Microeconomics exam.

SCORING YOUR PRACTICE TESTS

How do I score my practice tests?

The CLEP Principles of Microeconomics exam is scored on a scale of 20 to 80. To score your practice tests, count up the number of correct answers. This is your total raw score. Convert your raw score to a scaled score using the conversion table on the following page. (Note: The conversion table provides only an estimate of your scaled score. Scaled scores can and do vary over time, and in no case should a sample test be taken as a precise predictor of test performance. Nonetheless, our scoring table allows you to judge your level of performance within a reasonable scoring range.)

When will I receive my score report?

The test administrator will print out a full Candidate Score Report for you immediately upon your completion of the exam (except for CLEP English Composition with Essay). Your scores are reported only to you, unless you ask to have them sent elsewhere. If you want your scores reported to a college or other institution, you must say so when you take the examination. Since your scores are kept on file for 20 years, you can also request transcripts from Educational Testing Service at a later date.

STUDYING FOR THE CLEP

It is very important for you to choose the time and place for studying that works best for you. Some students may set aside a certain number of hours every morning, while others may choose to study at night before going to sleep. Other students may study during the day, while waiting on a line, or even while eating lunch. Only you can determine when and where your study time will be most effective. But be consistent and use your time wisely. Work out a study routine and stick to it!

PRACTICE-TEST RAW SCORE CONVERSION TABLE *

Raw Score	Scaled Score	Course Grade	Raw Score	Scaled Score	Course Grade
80	80	A	39	51	C
79	80	A	38	50	C
78	80	A	37	50	C
77	79	A	36	49	D
76	79	A	35	48	D
75	78	A	34	47	D
74	78	A	33	46	D
73	77	A	32	46	D
72	77	A	31	45	D
71	76	A	30	44	D
70	76	A	29	43	D
69	75	A	28	42	D
68	74	A	27	42	D
67	74	A	26	41	D
66	73	A	25	40	D
65	72	A	24	39	F
64	71	A	23	38	F
63	70	A	22	38	F
62	70	A	21	37	F
61	69	B	20	36	F
60	68	B	19	35	F
59	67	B	18	34	F
58	66	B	17	34	F
57	66	B	16	33	F
56	65	B	15	32	F
55	64	B	14	31	F
54	63	B	13	30	F
53	62	B	12	30	F
52	62	B	11	29	F
51	61	B	10	28	F
50	60	C	9	27	F
49	59	C	8	26	F
48	58	C	7	26	F
47	58	C	6	25	F
46	57	C	5	24	F
45	56	C	4	23	F
44	55	C	3	22	F
43	54	C	2	21	F
42	54	C	1	20	F
41	53	C	0	20	F
40	52	C			

*This table is provided for scoring REA practice tests only. The American Council on Education recommends that colleges use a single across-the-board credit-granting score of 50 for all CLEP computer-based exams. Nonetheless, on account of the different skills being measured and the unique content requirements of each test, the actual number of correct answers needed to reach 50 will vary. A 50 is calibrated to equate with performance that would warrant the grade C in the corresponding introductory college course.

When you take the practice tests, try to make your testing conditions as much like the actual test as possible. Turn your television and radio off, and sit down at a quiet table free from distraction. Make sure to time yourself. Start off by setting a timer for the time that is allotted for each section, and be sure to reset the timer for the appropriate amount of time when you start a new section.

As you complete each practice test, score your test and thoroughly review the explanations to the questions you answered incorrectly; however, do not review too much at one time. Concentrate on one problem area at a time by reviewing the question and explanation, and by studying our review until you are confident that you completely understand the material.

Test-Taking Tips

Although you may not be familiar with computer-based standardized tests such as the CLEP Principles of Microeconomics exam, there are many ways to acquaint yourself with this type of examination and to help alleviate your test-taking anxieties. Listed below are ways to help you become accustomed to the CLEP, some of which may be applied to other standardized tests as well.

Read all of the possible answers. Just because you think you have found the correct response, do not automatically assume that it is the best answer. Read through each choice to be sure that you are not making a mistake by jumping to conclusions.

Use the process of elimination. Go through each answer to a question and eliminate as many of the answer choices as possible. By eliminating just two answer choices, you give yourself a better chance of getting the item correct, since there will only be three choices left from which to make your guess. Remember, your score is based only on the number of questions you answer correctly.

Work quickly and steadily. You will have only 90 minutes to work on 80 questions, so work quickly and steadily to avoid focusing on any one question too long. Taking the practice tests in this book will help you learn to budget your time.

Acquaint yourself with the computer screen. Familiarize yourself with the CLEP computer screen beforehand by logging on to the College Board website. Waiting until test day to see what it looks like in the pretest tutorial risks experiencing needless anxiety into your testing experience.

Also, familiarizing yourself with the directions and format of the exam will save you valuable time on the day of the actual test.

Be sure that your answer registers before you go to the next item. Look at the screen to see that your mouse-click causes the pointer to darken the proper oval. This takes less effort than darkening an oval on paper, but don't lull yourself into taking less care!

THE DAY OF THE EXAM

Preparing for the CLEP

On the day of the test, you should wake up early (hopefully after a decent night's rest) and have a good breakfast. Make sure to dress comfortably, so that you are not distracted by being too hot or too cold while taking the test. Also plan to arrive at the test center early. This will allow you to collect your thoughts and relax before the test, and will also spare you the anxiety that comes with being late. As an added incentive to make sure you arrive early, keep in mind that no one will be allowed into the test session after the test has begun.

Before you leave for the test center, make sure that you have your admission form and another form of identification, which must contain a recent photograph, your name, and signature (i.e., driver's license, student identification card, or current alien registration card). You will not be admitted to the test center if you do not have proper identification.

If you would like, you may wear a watch to the test center. However, you may not wear one that makes noise, because it may disturb the other test-takers. No dictionaries, textbooks, notebooks, briefcases, or packages will be permitted and drinking, smoking, and eating are prohibited.

Good luck on the CLEP Principles of Microeconomics exam!

BASIC ECONOMIC CONCEPTS REVIEW

Basic Economic Concepts Review

KEY TERMS:

- Scarcity
- Needs and Wants
- Origin of Economics
- Economic Choice
- Trade-offs
- PPF Curve
- Law of Diminishing Marginal Returns
- Law of Increasing Opportunity Cost
- Laws of Supply and Demand
- Determinants of Supply
- Determinants of Demand
- Change in Quantity Supplied or Demanded
- Change in Supply or Demand
- Markets
- Equilibrium Price
- Shortage
- Surplus
- Productive Efficiency
- Allocative Efficiency
- Market Equilibrium
- Four Factors of Production (Inputs)
- Types of Economic Systems
- Circular Flow Model

ECONOMIC FOUNDATIONS

The study of economics involves a specific way of looking at how things work in the world. This approach has three main components: economic methods, macroeconomics, and microeconomics. Adam Smith is considered the "founding father" of economics, and his book, *The Wealth of Nations*, presented many of the concepts upon which this course is based. Since his work was published (in 1776), many others have furthered the study of economics, though they certainly have not always agreed with Smith. In fact, four general—and differing—viewpoints have evolved regarding the workings of markets: Classical, Keynesian, Monetary, and Neo-classical.

Microeconomics: Basic Economic Concepts

The study of microeconomics requires students to understand that, in any economy, the existence of limited resources along with unlimited wants results in the need to make choices. An effective economics course begins by studying the concepts of opportunity costs and trade-offs, which can be illustrated by the production possibilities curve or other analytical examples. The course can then proceed to a consideration of how different types of economies determine which goods and services to produce, how to produce them, and to whom to distribute them.

It is also important that students understand why and how specialization and exchange increase the total output of goods and services. In this context students need to be able to differentiate between absolute and comparative advantage, to identify comparative advantage from differences in output levels and labor costs, and to determine the basis under which mutually advantageous trade can take place between countries. Specific examples from actual economic situations can be used to illustrate and reinforce the principles involved.

Scarcity and Economic Choice

Economics is always about limits. We are, by the very nature of our existence, limited to the resources provided by the planet. Our wants and needs, however, are not limited, and therein lies the rub! The result is scarcity, the fundamental reality of economics. Because of scarcity, humankind must engage in production choices. The primary decision asks: Which of our needs and wants do we satisfy, and which go unfulfilled? Answering this question forces people to make choices, and trade-offs result. Economists help us to understand these choices and the variety of possibilities that we face. Economists employ models that help us to focus on specific relationships that exist in the production and consumption of goods and services. These models employ the scientific method, in that they apply logical analysis based on economic principles to predict and explain outcomes, as well as suggest policies.

Trade-offs and Opportunity Cost

Another basic observation of economics is that the economic choices we make result in trade-offs that can be measured. As those trade-offs are measured, we realize that various combinations of goods and services can be produced. However, as we produce more of one good, we incur a cost, in the form of lost production of an alternative good or service. The PPF Curve, the Law of Diminishing Marginal Returns, and the Law of Increasing Opportunity Cost help us to understand this axiom. Together, these realities govern the behavior of the supplier in the free market system. Let's start our review with a look at the PPF Curve.

Production Possibilities Frontier (PPF) Curve

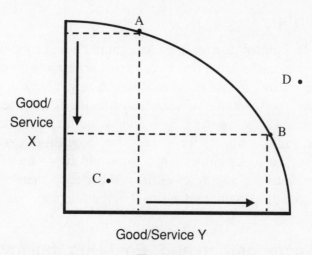

Good/Service Y

Figure 1

Figure 1 shows that as you move from point A to point B along the production curve, the quantity of Y produced increases, but the quantity of X decreases. In other words, you sacrifice X to gain Y. This is termed *opportunity cost*. The curve is bowed outward to represent the economic reality that as an input of production is used up, its output diminishes. The reverse of this procedure, a sacrifice of Y in order to produce more X, is possible as well. The curve represents the maximum possible combinations available. It is possible for an economy to produce inside the curve at C, a point that represents underusage of production inputs. The point of production represented by D is not possible given the current inputs (resources) present in the economy; to achieve D would require economic growth resulting from an increase in the inputs of production.

Theoretical Economics

Economists develop models of behavior focused on the forces that produce goods and services and those who consume them. Due to the complexity of the innumerable variable forces at work in the real world, economists attempt to reduce the study at hand to those facts they deem most relevant. In doing so, they attempt to develop hypotheses (such as cause and effect relationships) that lead them to generalize and develop principles or laws that predict probable outcomes of economic actions. Several key elements are necessary to assist in the formation of economic models and laws.

ECONOMIC METHODOLOGY

Ceteris Paribus

In order to simplify the topic under examination, economists use the "all other things equal" assumption to construct generalizations. This eliminates the impact that changes in other variables might have upon the topic being examined. For example, if we are examining the impact that a rise in oil prices would have on the U.S. economy and our currency values in particular, we would eliminate the impact that those oil prices would have on other nations' currency values. Thus, we could conclude that the dollar would appreciate as the supply of dollars in currency markets would decrease due to a decline in our real national output/income.

Fallacy of composition and "Post Hoc" fallacy

Additionally, two other pitfalls that economists must be wary of are the fallacy of composition and the "Post Hoc" fallacy, as they interfere with sound reasoning. The fallacy of composition simply means that one must not assume that what applies in one instance is true for the whole. For example, if you go to a comedy club and you find the first comic to be hilarious, it would be faulty to assume that all of the comics that night will be equally hilarious! The "Post Hoc" fallacy simply supposes that if one event follows another, the former is the cause of the latter. For example, to conclude that the sun rises due to the crowing of a rooster would certainly heighten the importance of roosters to our survival.

Marginal Analysis

Finally, a major analytical tool employed by economists is marginal analysis. Simply put marginal analysis entails the impact of one or more variables upon an economic outcome. For example, if a firm hired one more employee, how much would the output of the firm increase or decrease? The use of marginality helps economists predict decision making in the economy as one can determine a marginal benefit or a marginal cost relationship. With this in mind, it is easy to understand the use of graphs by economists in their study of economic relationships. A graph allows economists to quantify and record the relationship between two variables on the X (independent variable) and Y (dependent variable) axis. The positive or negative slope that results from the plotting of data reveals a general direct (positive, upward slope) or indirect (negative, downward slope) relationship. The calculation of the slope of the variables linear relationship is also very significant in predicting the infinite outcome of various combinations of two items.

ORIGINS OF SUPPLY

Law of Diminishing Marginal Returns

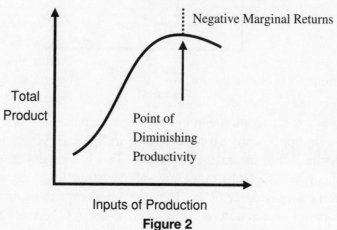

Figure 2

The model in figure 2 shows the relationship between the inputs of production and the total production resulting from those inputs. The inputs of production are: raw material, labor, capital (money or goods), and entrepreneurship. Initially, as we increase the factors of production, output increases at an increasing rate. At some point, however, additional inputs not only create output at a diminishing rate, but actually decrease the total output. The production table (table 1) demonstrates that relationship. Notice that as the third input is added to production, the total output increases from 12 to 16, but the marginal rate of change has decreased from 7 units gained to only 4 units of gained production. This is a diminishing rate, hence the name *Law of Diminishing Marginal Returns*. When the fifth input is added, the total productivity actually decreases from 16 to 12, a loss of 4 units.

Table 1

Input	1	2	3	4	5
Output	5	12	16	16	12

Law of Increasing Opportunity Costs

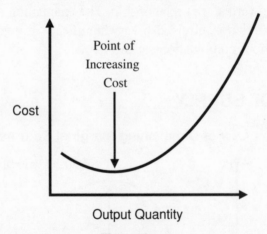

Figure 3

There is a clear relationship between the decrease in productivity and the increase in opportunity cost. As shown in figure 3, when productivity diminishes, the cost of production increases. This is what governs the law of supply and is why the graph slopes upward. A change in price causes movement along the supply curve. Why? Because a higher price covers the higher cost of increased production; more product is brought to market. Figure 4 shows this direct relationship.

Determinants of Supply

Determinants of supply (that is, the prices of raw materials, labor, capital, and entrepreneurship) may cause the curve to shift (see figure 5). An increase in the price of the inputs of production causes a contraction in supply. This is shown as an upward and leftward movement of the supply curve. If input prices decrease, the supply curve moves downward and to the right, representing an overall increase in supply. Because the producer's cost of production begins to increase at some point, a producer must receive a higher sales price to be induced to make additional product. Remember, a producer is driven by profit, and maximum profit is the goal. Therefore, producers seek minimum cost per unit of production for the highest productive efficiency.

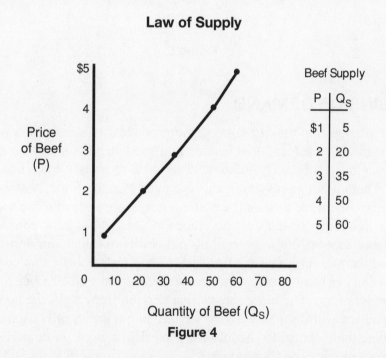

Law of Supply

Beef Supply

P	Q_S
$1	5
2	20
3	35
4	50
5	60

Figure 4

If the determinants of supply reduce the cost of production, the supply curve shifts from S_1 to S_2 (as shown in figure 5). This shift represents an overall increase in the quantity of goods brought to market at lower prices. If the determinants of supply increase the cost of production, the supply curve shifts from S_3 to S_1. This change in supply represents a decrease in the quantity of goods brought to market at higher prices.

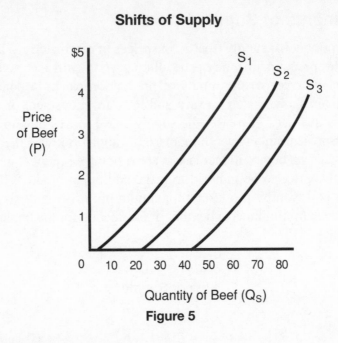

Shifts of Supply

Quantity of Beef (Q$_S$)
Figure 5

ORIGINS OF DEMAND

Increasing opportunity costs cause producers to behave in a predict-able manner. Consumers also behave in a predictable manner because of scarcity. Consumers seek goods and services to satisfy their needs and wants. Though our needs and wants are unlimited, both the existence and the availability of the economic resources necessary to meet those needs are limited. Economic systems are developed to address this basic conflict. In a free market system, our income limits our ability to satisfy our desires (this is called the *rationing power* of prices). Economists believe that consumer satisfaction can be measured, since consumers attach a dollar value to goods and services (g/s). The more satisfaction derived from a g/s, the higher the price you are willing to pay. When we measure a group of consumers, we determine their demand schedule for a particular item. Price serves as a means of rationing the g/s produced.

Figure 6 is a graphic model of a demand table for good X. At a low price of $1, consumers are willing to buy 80 units; when the price rises to $2, consumers demand fewer units, 55. Notice that a change in price causes a change in the quantity demanded. The relationship between a change in price and a change in quantity demanded is a basic economic understanding. A primary feature of demand is that as price rises, the quantity demanded falls; and as price falls, the quantity demanded increases. Economists call

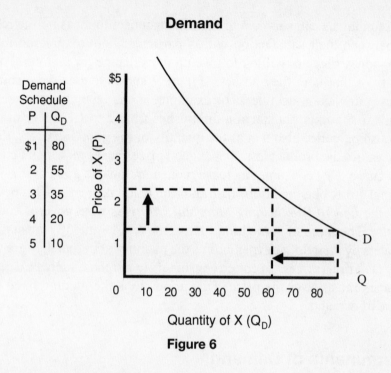

Figure 6

this inverse relationship the *Law of Demand*. Why is this inverse relation-ship always present in consumer behavior? The primary answer stems from the nature of humankind, established in the law of diminishing marginal utility.

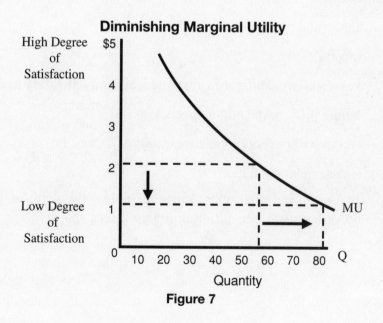

Figure 7

Economists can survey a group of consumers to measure the relationship between their satisfaction with a particular item (expressed in terms of the money they are willing to give up in exchange for that item) and the quantity of that item they possess. Figure 7 shows that as the quantity increases, satisfaction declines. For example, as the quantity increases from 55 units to 80 units, satisfaction diminishes from 2 to 1. This is an inverse relationship. Notice also that as the quantity of the good increases, the consumer values the product less; a change in price causes movement along the utility curve. As a consumer increases consumption of a good or service, the marginal utility obtained from each additional unit decreases. This principle, called the *Law of Diminishing Marginal Utility*, is what governs consumer behavior. The more of something I have, the less I value it. Consumers tell producers by their dollar expenditures the quantity of output they are willing to buy at various prices. To entice consumers to purchase increased quantity, producers must lower the price. This principle is the guiding hand behind the law of demand.

Determinants of Demand

Finally, because consumer (sovereignty) demand may change at any time (figure 8), the entire schedule may shift outward (D_2 to D_3) signaling greater demand; or inward (D_2 to D_1), indicating less demand. These changes in demand are caused by a group of factors called the *determinants of demand*:

- Tastes and preferences

- Income

- Price and availability of substitute and complementary goods

- Future price or quantity expectations

- Number of buyers (population size)

- Government regulation

So, for example, if red shirts became trendy, the demand for red shirts would shift outward, resulting in higher prices and greater quantity bought.

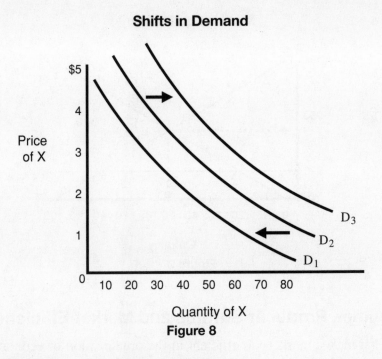

Shifts in Demand

Figure 8

THE NATURE AND FUNCTION OF PRODUCT MARKETS

Determining Price and Quantity

The forces of supply and demand come together in the marketplace. The market is a mechanism, a place where buyers and sellers of goods and services meet to satisfy their self-interest. The invisible forces of supply and demand interact to determine the price and quantity of goods bought and sold in the marketplace. The model portrayed in figure 9 assumes that competition is present for both producers and consumers. Free markets seek a balance between the interests of buyer and seller. This compromise point is known as the *equilibrium price*. It is the point at which supply and demand intersect. Equilibrium is significant, for it is at this price and quantity that the market clears, the price stabilizes, and product is available. Move from this price or quantity, and either shortage (inadequate supply of goods) or surplus (excess unsold goods) results. Economists have developed a graphic model of this event.

Market Equilibrium

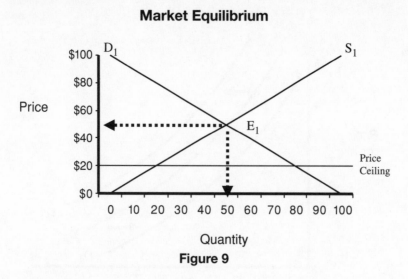

Figure 9

Consumer, Producer Surplus and Market Efficiency

What makes markets so efficient in the organization of economic activity is the role of consumer and producer surplus. Consumer surplus as depicted in Figure 10 refers to the portion of the demand curve that lies above the equilibrium point. This portion of the demand curve represents those consumers that value the good so highly they would be willing to pay a higher price to attain it. Thus, any rise in price would reduce consumer surplus and any fall in price would increase consumer surplus.

Producer surplus (Figure 10) refers to those suppliers that would be willing to bring their goods to market at an even lower price. Any rise in price would increase producer surplus and a fall in price would decrease it. When the consumer surplus and the producer surplus are added together the total surplus that represents the total benefit to society from the production and consumption of the good is realized. Notice that maximum total surplus is present at equilibrium.

Reallocation Reduces Surplus

In Figure 11, Consumer A is willing to pay $4.00 per lb. for beef, while Consumer D is only willing to pay $2.00 per lb. If we take beef from A and give it to D, consumer surplus would decline from $4.00 to $2.00. Simply put, A has had a highly valued good taken away and given to another that values it less. Thus, total surplus of satisfaction declines by $2.00 and the total benefit to society would decline as well.

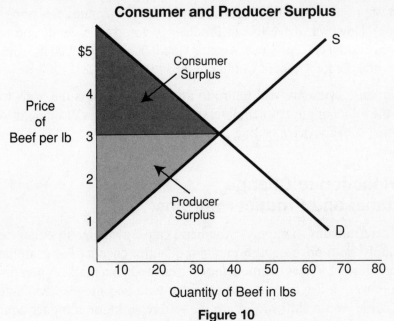

Figure 10

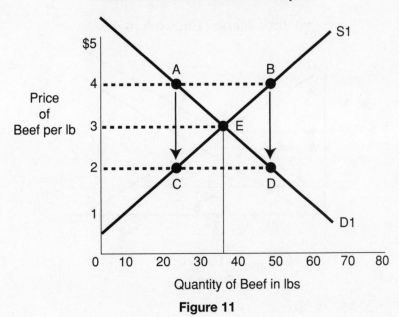

Figure 11

Now view Figure 11 from the producer standpoint. Assume that Producer B has a cost of $4.00 per lb while Producer C has a cost of $2.00 per lb. At an equilibrium price of $3.00 per lb, Producer C would provide the market with beef (the cost of production is less than sales price = profit/happy) and

25

Producer B would not (the cost of production is higher than the sales price = loss/unhappy). However, if we forced Producer B to provide goods and reduced sales by Producer C, producer surplus would decline by $2.00 as would total surplus and the total benefit would fall by $2.00 as well.

Later in this review we will return to this concept as it is the basis for analysis of the effect of government intervention into markets through introduction of tax, subsidy, price ceiling and floor.

Market Reaction to Change in Consumer and Producer Surplus

If the determinants of supply or demand cause a change in either demand or supply, both price equilibrium and quantity change. For example, let's say that figure 12 shows the model for the canned tuna market operating at E_1. If there were a fish disease outbreak and tuna became less available, the supply curve would shift inward, to the left, resulting in a higher equilibrium price of tuna and lower equilibrium quantity at E_2.

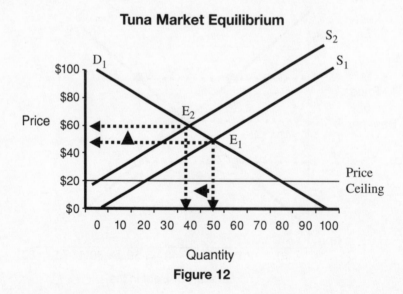

Tuna Market Equilibrium

Figure 12

Four Resource Inputs

In markets, the forces of supply and demand are constantly at work. Economic systems organize society's decisions regarding the use of resources. Production of all goods and services requires four main resource inputs:

1. Land—raw materials.

2. Capital—means of production (investment goods) and finance capital (money used to acquire capital goods).

3. Labor—human resources, including both manual and intellectual skills.

4. Entrepreneurship—business organization and/or innovation.

Four Main Economic Systems

Over the years, humankind has organized the means and distribution of production into four economic system types. Those systems are:

1. Free market—consumers and producers operate in an unregulated environment.

2. Traditional—society does not change its methods of production or consumption.

3. Command (state centrally planned)—government agencies regulate production and consumption.

4. Mixed market—system blends free market, traditional, and state planning. (In recent years the mixed market system has become increasingly prevalent as the command economies have failed (USSR) or modified (China) by adapting more free market features.)

All of these systems hold in common the need to answer the same three basic questions:

1. Which goods and services to produce?

2. How to produce goods and services?

3. To whom to distribute the goods and services?

CIRCULAR FLOW MODEL

Today, nearly all of the world's nations employ some form of the market system. It is critical that we understand the key decision makers and main markets present in this system, which is governed by supply and demand. The circular flow model (figure 13) helps us to see the two main decision makers in a free market: Households and Businesses.

Consumer and Producer

The two main markets where these two groups interact are the *resource* (input factor) *market* and the *product market*. Input resources flow from the Household to Businesses in the resource market. This purchase of input from the Household is the cost of production to a business. The sale of these resources by Households to Businesses generates Household income (wages, rents, interest, and profits). Remember, one of the key features of a free market economy is that the means (inputs) of production are owned by the individual. The product market is the place where Businesses sell their goods and services to Households. This sale to the Household is the source of a Business's revenue. When a Business subtracts its costs from this revenue, profit/loss is determined. This consumption of goods and services by Households is where the income earned from the resource market is expended. When a Household subtracts its consumption expenditures from its income, savings or debt are determined.

Circular Flow Model

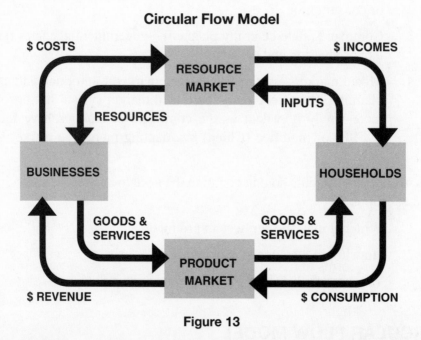

Figure 13

Now add the public sector of Government to the private sector of Households and Businesses (figure 14) on the circular flow model. Notice that the Government purchases goods and services from the product market and employs input factors from the resource market. These purchases are the origin of our public goods, such as roads and bridges. Government finances its purchases through taxation of the private sector. This flow of goods, services, and tax dollars (subsidy and transfer payments) suggests how Government might try, through fiscal policy, to stabilize the economy.

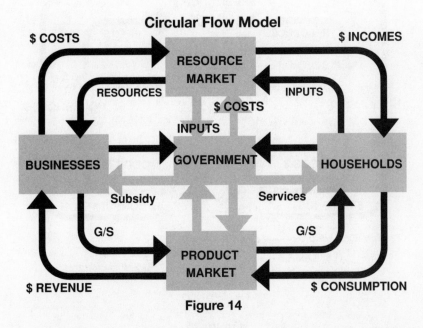

Circular Flow Model

Figure 14

Today, the majority of the world's nations have agreed to follow many of these principles, and joined together in the World Trade Organization. This organization has contributed to increased specialization in the world, creating greater productive efficiency. Nations today seek absolute or comparative advantage in production, resulting in greater trade and thus increasing their standard of living. This freer international trade has greatly increased global competition, which affects a large number of U.S. firms. The supporters and critics of free trade continue to debate the advantages and disadvantages of this mixed market system. Nonetheless, imports and exports play a role in our economy. Imports and exports are the final link in the chain that forms our economy (figure 15). To see this, we return to the circular flow model for a last time.

Notice in figure 15 that when the United States exports goods and services to the rest of the world, wealth from those other nations flows into ours. The opposite is also true: when we purchase foreign goods and services (import), our wealth flows into the foreign producer. This forms the basis for the balance of trade (examined in greater detail later). Essentially, exports add to our wealth (favorable balance of trade) while imports subtract from our wealth (unfavorable balance of trade). Also note that imports increase goods and services available for domestic consumption.

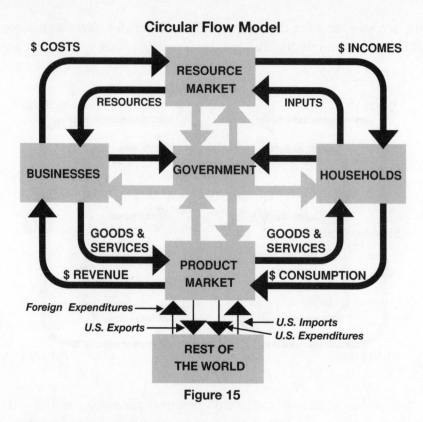

Circular Flow Model

Figure 15

Free Market Economy Principles

The United States has a mixed market economy, primarily employing free market principles. Among the most important characteristics of a market system are:

- private property

- freedom to enter or exit production markets

- freedom to dispose of your property as you see fit

- freedom to work in any area for which you are qualified

- freedom to buy goods and services that satisfy your wants

- freedom to act in your own self-interest

- competition among producers

- competition among consumers

- specialization/division of labor

- presence of a money system

- government provision of legal framework, enforcement, and infrastructure

This last point creates issues of market failure, spillover benefits and costs, public goods, transfer payments, taxation, and regulation, among others.

The nature and degree of government intervention into our economy causes constant, and often heated, debate in the United States. All government spending (unless financed by foreign capital inflows) is financed through taxation of the consumer or producer and reduces their disposable income (seen as a leakage). This flow of goods, services, and tax dollars suggests how government tries, through fiscal policy, to stabilize the economy.

CLEP
MICROECONOMICS
COURSE REVIEW

Microeconomics Review

KEY TERMS:

- Price elasticity
  - Elastic
  - Inelastic
- Total revenue and elasticity
- Cross elasticity of demand
- Cross elasticity of income
- Price ceiling
- Price floor
- Price elasticity of supply
- Consumer utility maximization and budget income limits
- Explicit cost
- Implicit cost
- Short run
- Long run
- TFC, TVC, AFC, AVC, ATC, MC
- Economy of scale
- Least cost (output and input analysis)
- Maximum Profit (Output and Input analysis)
- Four market models:
  - Pure competition
  - Monopoly (imperfect competition)
  - Monopolistic competition
  - Oligopoly (shared monopoly)
  - Game Theory
  - Strategic Behavior
- Cartel
- Marginal product
- Marginal revenue product
- Marginal resource cost
- Monopsony
- Union effect

- Minimum wage
- Lorenz curve
- Taxation
  - Progressive
  - Proportional
  - Regressive
- Deadweight loss
- Transfer payment
- Public goods
- Spillover cost and benefit
- Merger
  - Horizontal
  - Vertical
  - Conglomerate

THE NATURE AND FUNCTIONS OF PRODUCT MARKETS

The study of the nature and functions of product markets covers three broad areas.

The Interaction of Market Supply and Demand

A well-planned microeconomics course requires an analysis of the determinants of supply and demand and the ways in which changes in these determinants affect supply and demand curves. In particular, the course helps students make the important distinction between movements along the curves and shifts in the curves themselves. The course should also emphasize the process by which equilibrium price and quantity are determined and the impact of government policies such as price floors and ceilings, excise taxes, tariffs, and quotas.

The Theory of Consumer Choice

Students should learn that consumers choose goods in the market to maximize satisfaction. By examining the demand side of the product market, students learn how incomes, prices, and tastes affect consumer purchases. Here it is important that students gain an understanding of how the income and substitution effects determine the shape of the demand curve, how an individual's demand curve is derived, and how the individual and market demand curves are related. Students are also expected to study the characteristics that determine the price elasticity of demand and to apply the concept of elasticity to the analysis of real-world problems.

The Supply Side of the Product Market

By examining the theory of the firm, the course introduces discussion of a firm's economic costs. This discussion includes an analysis of the relationship between diminishing returns and marginal costs; the relationships between total, average, and marginal costs in the long run and in the short run; and the behavior of firms in different types of market structures. In its discussion of perfect competition, the course focuses on determining short-run and long-run equilibria, both for the profit-maximizing individual firm and for the industry; and on the equilibrium relationships between price, marginal and average revenues, marginal and average costs, and profits. In considering the market behavior of a monopolist, students compare a monopolist's price, level of output, and profit with those of a firm operating in a perfectly competitive market. By paying particular attention to the concept of allocative efficiency, students learn how and why competitive firms achieve an efficient allocation of resources, whereas monopolists do not. Students also learn why government should in some cases encourage competition and in others allow a regulated monopoly to exist. Lastly, well-prepared students will gain some familiarity with the characteristics of monopolistic competition and oligopoly and their effects on efficiency.

INTERACTION OF SUPPLY AND DEMAND

As we learned in the initial general review, economics is always about limits. Resources are limited, whereas our wants and needs are unlimited. The result is scarcity, which forces us to make consumption and production choices. Various combinations of goods and services (g/s) can be produced. However, as we produce more of one g/s, we incur a cost in the form of lost production of an alternative good or service. These forces underlie the laws of demand and supply. In microeconomics we will extend our investigation of those forces. Let's start our review with a look at the impact of changes in price on the buyers and sellers of a g/s. This is called *price elasticity*.

PRICE ELASTICITY OF DEMAND

We already know that consumers are governed by the law of diminishing marginal utility. Thus, they will buy more of a g/s only if its price declines. Elasticity gives us a quantitative means by which to measure this consumer sensitivity to price change. The simple test for elasticity gives us the formula:

$$E_d = \frac{\% \text{ change in quantity demanded of g/s A}}{\% \text{ change in price of g/s A}}$$

This calculation yields a percentage outcome that allows us to compare consumer behavior across product types and prices. Economists use the following benchmarks to classify the nature of the price elasticity quotient:

- If $E_d > 1$, then demand is elastic.
- If $E_d < 1$, then demand is inelastic.
- If $E_d = 1$, the demand is unitary elastic.

The minus or plus sign of the change is irrelevant, as we are concerned only with the amount of change, not whether it is an increase or a decrease. For example, let's say that the price of a soft drink increased by 20% and the demand changed by 40%.

$$E_d = 0.40/0.20 = 2 > 1, \text{ therefore demand is elastic}$$

This demand is classified as elastic or flexible because consumers showed greater sensitivity to price than to quantity of product demanded. In other words, the consumer was more concerned with the price than with the g/s. If consumers behaved in the opposite manner, we would consider their demand to be inelastic or inflexible.

$$E_d = 0.20/0.40 = 0.5 < 1, \text{ therefore demand is inelastic}$$

In this case, consumers have demonstrated a greater concern for the product than for the price. Without question, producers of g/s are very interested in customers' reaction to price changes. Remember, the consumer (sovereignty) is king.

Unitary elasticity occurs when the consumer is equally concerned with price and product. Unitary elasticity is demonstrated as:

$$E_d = 0.50/0.50 = 1, \text{ therefore demand is unitary elastic}$$

Extreme cases of consumer reaction to price are termed *perfectly inelastic* if the price coefficient is near zero. This represents a g/s that is so needed by the consumer that it is a necessity for life, such as insulin to a diabetic. This is drawn as a line perpendicular to the horizontal axis (figure 1).

The other extreme case of consumer reaction to price is called *perfectly elastic*, if the price coefficient is significantly greater than 1. This repre-

Perfectly Inelastic Demand

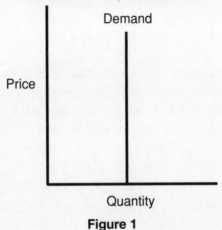

Figure 1

Perfectly Elastic Demand

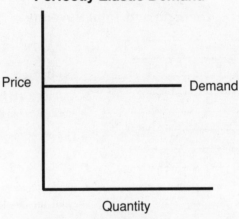

Figure 2

sents a g/s that is completely unnecessary to the consumer—a luxury. This is drawn as a line perpendicular to the vertical axis (figure 2).

One of the limitations of the simple test for elasticity is that, depending on which portion of a demand curve you measure, the outcome coefficient will be elastic in the upper left portion and inelastic in the lower right half. Calculating the slope of the demand curve could also be misleading, as you would be measuring absolute change over the entire demand for the product. Elasticity, in contrast, seeks relative changes in price and quantity. A more accurate measure of consumer elasticity is the total revenue curve. This more precise determination of total revenue is of great importance to a firm as it affects maximization of its profitability.

THE TOTAL REVENUE TEST

Total revenue is defined as price multiplied by quantity:

$$TR = P \times Q$$

Total revenue calculation allows a firm to determine whether a price intersects demand in the elastic or inelastic portion of the demand curve. If the price intersects the elastic portion of the demand curve then there will be an inverse relationship between price and revenue. This means that if price decreases and quantity demanded increases resulting in an increase in total revenue, the firm would be operating in the elastic portion of the curve. If a price decrease causes a decline in total revenue, even though the firm has increased sales, the firm would be operating in the portion of the demand curve that would be classified as inelastic. The impact of the total revenue test is best viewed graphically (figure 3).

Demand and Total Revenue

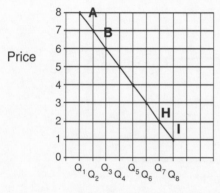

Price

Quantity Demanded

- At A, TR = $8 \times 1 = \$8$

- At B, TR = $7 \times 2 = \$14$
- An increase in total revenue indicates elasticity of demand.

- At H, TR = $2 \times 7 = \$14$

- At I, TR = $1 \times 8 = \$8$

- A decrease in total revenue indicates inelasticity of demand.

Figure 3

This method of measuring consumer reaction to price changes is most useful when the results are plotted to show the changes in a firm's total revenue. Notice that at some point, the sale of one more unit is detrimental to the firm's total revenue, because to sell that good, the firm has to lower the price so much that the total revenue actually declines. Why would a firm want to sell that extra good if it will lose revenue by making the sale? In general, it won't. Firms want to maximize profit. As we will see in the four market models, however, if the cost curve for a firm is such that its costs are minimized in the inelastic portion of the demand curve, then profit maximization would dictate (depending on the level of competition present in the market) that it operate in the inelastic portion of the demand curve.

Price Elasticity and Total Revenue Curve

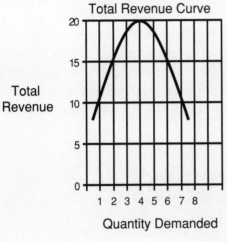

- This allows us to see that there is indeed a maximum revenue point.
- Selling more product beyond Q4 actually decreases revenues and thus profits.

Figure 4

When the fourth unit is sold, total revenue is maximized. If the fifth unit is sold, total revenue declines.

In figure 5, we align the demand curve from figure 3 with the total revenue curve from figure 4. The different ranges of elasticity become clear when we employ the total revenue test to find the elastic and inelastic portions of the demand curve. Clearly after a price of $4.00 any further lowering of price (even though more units are sold) results in a decline in total revenue for a firm.

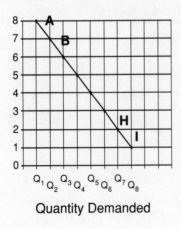

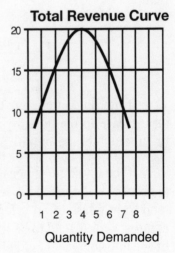

Figure 5

CROSS ELASTICITY OF DEMAND

The cross elasticity formula gives us additional insight into consumer behavior. This aspect of consumer behavior is of great importance to producers in determining what quantity of g/s to produce. Sellers anticipate the impact of price changes on the quantity demand of a g/s by gauging the effect on the total revenue the firm will generate. Cross elasticity (denoted as E_{ab}) also builds on the concepts of substitute and complementary g/s. The formula is:

$$E_{ab} = \frac{\% \text{ of change in the } Q_d \text{ of g/s A}}{\% \text{ of change in price of g/s A}}$$

If the quotient is positive, then the g/s are substitutes for each other. For example, if Jiffy peanut butter increases in price and the sale of Peter Pan peanut butter increases, then consumers have reacted to the increase in the price of Jiffy by changing to Peter Pan.

If the coefficient is negative, the products are used together and are complements to each other. If ice cream increases in price and the quantity of fudge topping demanded decreases, the price of one has affected the demand for the other. If the goods are unrelated, a zero or near-zero outcome results.

Income elasticity of demand determines and classifies the relationship between income and demand for a g/s. The formula for income elasticity of demand is:

$$E_{income} = \frac{\% \text{ of change in the quantity demanded}}{\% \text{ of change in income}}$$

If the outcome is positive, then an increase in income has resulted in an increase in the quantity demanded. This indicates that the g/s is normal or superior (brand-name).

If the outcome is negative, then a decrease in income has increased the purchase of the g/s. This is an inferior g/s, for as income increases people tend to buy less of an inferior g/s (generic label). However, as income decreases, people tend to be forced, by income budget constraints, to buy more of an inferior g/s. This helps explain why consumers, during a recession, continue to buy staples, such as food, but forgo durable goods such as electronics or automobiles.

PRICE ELASTICITY OF SUPPLY

We already know that producers are governed by the law of increasing opportunity cost (because they seek maximum profit or least loss). Thus, they will supply one more unit of good only if the sale price rises enough to cover the increased cost of production. The formula to determine elasticity of supply is basically the same as for demand.

$$E_s = \frac{\% \text{ of change in the } Q_s \text{ of g/s}}{\% \text{ of change in the price of g/s}}$$

Economists use the following benchmarks to classify the degree of elasticity present for the g/s:

- If $E_s > 1$, then supply is elastic.
- If $E_s < 1$, then supply is inelastic.
- If $E_s = 1$, then the supply is unit elastic.

Elasticity of supply raises the issue of long run, short run, and shelf life. If the life expectancy of the good is short, as for fresh fruits or vegetables, the supply will be perfectly inelastic. The producer is unable to alter supply and will sell at any price rather than take a total loss. In the short run, a plant's production capacity is fixed. This results in a relatively inelastic supply schedule, as the input factors cannot be recombined to shift supply. In the long run, however, factors can be recombined and a more elastic schedule can be attained. There is no total revenue test for elasticity of supply, as price and total revenue move in the same direction. The models depicting short-run inelastic supply and long-run elastic supply are shown in figure 6.

Elastic (Long-Run) and Inelastic (Short-Run) Supply

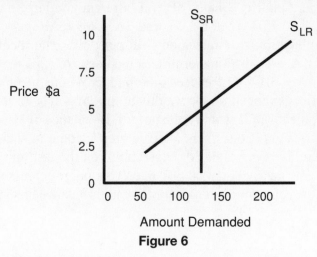

Amount Demanded

Figure 6

CONSUMER CHOICE

How do consumers choose goods and services in the marketplace? What effect does a change in income have on consumer behavior? For the most part, the laws of demand, price elasticity, and cross elasticity (already reviewed conceptually) answer these two questions. Remember that the law of demand is based on the law of diminishing marginal utility. Quantitative analysis, however, is both helpful and revealing. An algebraic statement helps us view the decision-making process from a utility maximization standpoint. Consumers want to allocate their disposable income in such a way that they balance the last dollar spent on a product with its utility yield. This process of utility maximization, in its simplest form, begins with allocation of consumer dollars between two products. The formula is:

$$\frac{\text{Marginal Utility of Product X}}{\text{Price of X}} = \frac{\text{Marginal Utility of Product Y}}{\text{Price of Y}}$$

When limited income and set prices are brought into play, the consumer will allocate income in such a way as to balance marginal utility per dollar for every good purchased, and will spend all income (we assume no borrowing or savings at this time). The maximum utility per dollar within an income limit modifies the formula as follows:

$$\frac{\text{Marginal Utility of Product X}}{\text{Price of X}} = \frac{\text{Marginal Utility of Product Y}}{\text{Price of Y}}$$

$$= \text{Income Limit}$$

Table 1 provides an illustration of this behavior. Notice that marginal utility (Mu) per dollar is equal at several different combinations: 1A + 4B (5Mu per $), 2A + 5B (4Mu per $), and 3A + 6B (3Mu per $). Only the 2A + 5B combination maximizes our Mu per dollar and income limit of $9. Note that 1A + 4B = $6 underutilizes income, 2A + 5B = $9 meets the budget, and 3A + 3B = $12 exceeds the budget. If our income, utility of product, or prices changed, so too would our mix of goods. If the number of g/s increased, the formula would still apply and a balance of Mu and income would still be sought. Consumers allocate their income in such a way that the marginal utilities per dollar of expenditure on the last unit of each g/s purchased are as nearly equal as possible. This point expresses consumer equilibrium; the consumer will not stray from this balance unless stimulated to do so.

Table 1

Units of Product A ($2)	Marginal Utility of A	Marginal Utility per Dollar	Units of Product B ($1)	Marginal Utility of B	Marginal Utility per Dollar
1	10	5	1	8	8
2	8	4	2	7	7
3	6	3	3	6	6
4	4	2	4	5	5
5	3	1.5	5	4	4
6	2	1	6	3	3

INCOME CONSTRAINTS AND BUDGET LIMITS

Income limits lead to budget analysis, which is another way to explain consumer choice and works along with the concept of marginal utility. The budget line itself displays the various combinations of g/s that a consumer is willing and able to buy at a particular income. A budget line is necessary to reveal the consumer's income level/budget. Any combination inward of the budget line is attainable; any area outside the budget line is unattainable (unless income increases). The consumer combination of goods is possible anywhere along the income limit line. In figure 7, points A (4 units of B, 1 unit of A) and B (4 units of A, 1 unit of B) represent two possible combinations of goods that meet budget limits.

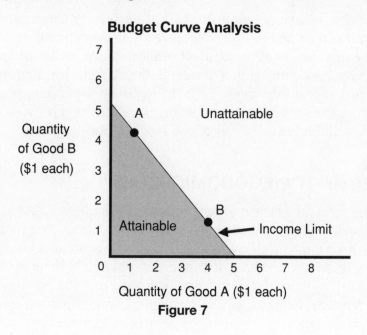

Budget Curve Analysis

Figure 7

If the income of the consumer or the price of the good changes, the budget line must be redrawn. For example, if the price of good B were reduced to $0.50, the new budget line would be as depicted in figure 8. Now the consumer can afford greater quantities at both point A (8 units of B and 1 of A) and point B (2 units of B and 4 units of A).

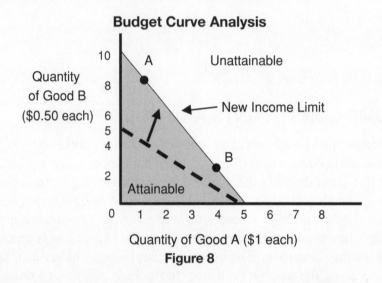

Figure 8

PRODUCER BEHAVIOR

Producer behavior is governed by self-interest. Producers seek maximum profit as their primary goal. Necessary to the understanding of a firm's profit is an awareness of the costs of production, consumer demand, revenue received, and competition present in the marketplace. Remember the circular flow model from figure 13 in the basic economic concepts review? A firm's decisions are based on the changing relationship between cost and revenue over different quantities of goods sold at various prices.

OPPORTUNITY (ECONOMIC) COST

Remember the concept of opportunity cost discussed at the beginning of this review. The more of an input employed by a firm in the production of a g/s, the greater the firm's cost in lost opportunity to produce an alternative g/s. Also, recall how the Law of Diminishing Marginal Returns (Marginal Productivity) explains the rising costs that occur at some point in the production schedule. Economists view economic cost in two ways, explicit and implicit costs. *Explicit (obvious) costs* are payments made to input resource suppliers. *Implicit (hidden) costs* are the lost opportunity of entrepreneurial talent and capital resources that were applied elsewhere. For example, suppose you are employed at a job that pays you $100,000 per year to design houses for a large construction firm. You decide to quit this job and start your own firm to custom-design homes. At the end of your first year, when all explicit costs are covered, you have a remainder of $50,000 of accounting profit. However, what about the forgone income from your previous efforts of $100,000? Haven't you lost $50,000 of former income? An economist would state that you have not had a normal profit unless you account for the forgone income from your previous job as an entrepreneurial (implicit) cost. So, economic profit is any amount above your explicit and implicit costs combined. This is a clear difference between the way an accountant and an economist define profit. In this particular example, an economist would say you incurred an economic loss of $50,000 (the amount that was less than your former salary).

PRODUCER TIME CONSTRAINTS

Demand for a firm's g/s can change quickly. A producer can be called upon by consumers to increase or decrease its production quantity at a moment's notice. Its profitability may depend on the time frame necessary to alter its inputs of production. Economists classify time into two key categories, short run and long run. Short run is a time period during which plant capacity to produce is said to be fixed or unchangeable. The inputs of production cannot be altered beyond a 24-hour-a-day, 7-day work week maximum. Long run is a time period during which plant capacity to produce is said to be changeable. All inputs of production can be altered, plants can be built or closed, and inputs can be added or reduced. Firms may enter or exit the industry altogether. No fixed amount of time defines short run or long run; it varies from industry to industry. Therefore, we see a difference in firms' short-run and long-run cost curves.

SHORT-RUN PRODUCTION COSTS

A firm must calculate all its costs of production before it can determine its profit/loss. First, a firm must pay for its input resources. These costs, which increase at some point, are variable costs (such as labor, energy, raw materials) that change at various levels of production. Firms also incur set costs. These fixed costs (such as rents, interest on debt, lost value of capital goods over time, insurance) must be paid regardless of whether a firm produces. When all these costs are added, we have a producer's total costs. Managers view the distinction between fixed and variable costs as significant, in that variable costs can be altered in the short run whereas fixed costs cannot. A firm that is unable to cover its variable costs must eventually shut down (unpaid workers will at some point seek employment elsewhere). Shut-down point is demonstrated graphically in figure 9.

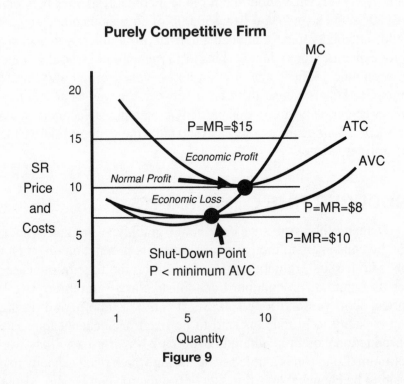

Figure 9

COST ANALYSIS

Producers are very interested in costs, as they are somewhat within the producers' control and determine a firm's very existence. Unit cost data, as depicted in figure 9, is meaningful in determining prices that must be charged at various levels of production to realize loss, normal, and economic profit points. Average fixed cost (AFC = TFC/Q), when plotted, shows that a firm's fixed costs decrease the most in the early stages of production quantity increase; even though a firm's fixed costs continuously decline, the rate of decline diminishes significantly. Average variable cost (AVC = TVC/Q) incorporates the law of diminishing returns: initial gains in productivity slow, opportunity costs rise, and average variable costs eventually increase. Average fixed cost and average variable cost, when added, give us the average total cost (ATC = AFC + AVC). Critical to a firm's decision to increase or decrease production is the concept of marginal cost. Marginal cost—the cost incurred by the last unit produced—is within a manager's control. Average cost figures do not give a manager the same specific information. Marginal cost is the additional cost of producing one more unit (MC = change in Total Cost / change in Quantity). Marginal cost is shaped by the same economic forces that shape average variable cost; that is, marginal productivity. At some point in the production of a good, marginal costs begin to increase, as marginal productivity peaks. They are mirror images. Productivity cost tables (see table 2) and graphic models are critical to portraying these concepts.

Table 2
Total, Average, and Marginal Cost Schedules in Short Run

Total Output	Total Fixed Costs	Total Variable Costs	Total Costs	Average Fixed Costs	Average Variable Costs	Average Total Costs	Marginal Costs
Q	TFC	TVC	$TC = TFC + TVC$	$AFC = \dfrac{TFC}{Q}$	$AVC = \dfrac{TVC}{Q}$	$ATC = \dfrac{TC}{Q}$	$MC = \dfrac{\Delta TC}{\Delta Q}$
0	$10	$0	$10				
1	10	10	20	$10	$10	$20	$10
2	10	18	28	5	9	14	8
3	10	25	35	3.33	8.33	11.6	7
4	10	30	40	2.5	7.5	10	5
5	10	35	45	2	7	9	5
6	10	42	52	1.66	7	8.66	7
7	10	50.6	60.6	1.44	7.2	8.6	8.6
8	10	60	70	1.25	7.5	8.75	9.4
9	10	80	90	1.1	8.8	10	20

- Note that AFC declines at a greater rate in the early stages of production.
- Note that AVC begins to increase after the sixth unit (diminishing marginal productivity).
- Note that ATC also increases after the seventh unit (cost decreases from AFC have a lesser impact than increases in AVC).
- Note that MC increases after the fifth unit of output.

The cost relationships expressed in table form can also be charted graphically, as in figure 10.

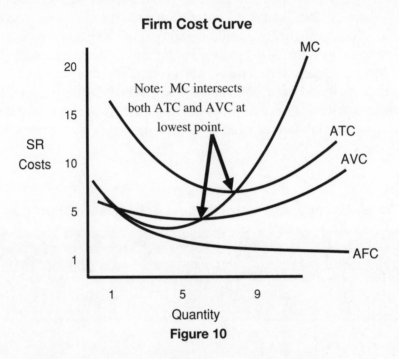

Firm Cost Curve

Note: MC intersects both ATC and AVC at lowest point.

MC

ATC

AVC

AFC

SR Costs

Quantity

Figure 10

LONG-RUN COSTS OF PRODUCTION

Long run is a time frame in which firms can alter all inputs of production. Also, other firms can enter or exit production in the long run, thereby increasing or decreasing industry output. Long-run cost curves are made up of segments of short-run ATC curves (see figure 11). Each short-run cost curve has a minimum ATC point; long-run cost curves connect the ATC curves' minimums. The long-run cost curves reveal the concept of economies of scale. Some industries (usually for durable goods) do not attain minimum ATC until a fairly high output level is attained. The auto industry is a prime example. However, there is still a limit to the cost savings obtainable by increasing scale, and eventually factors such as bureaucracy of management, worker alienation, and government regulation will cause costs to increase (diseconomies of scale).

Construction of Long-Run Cost Curve Economy of Scale

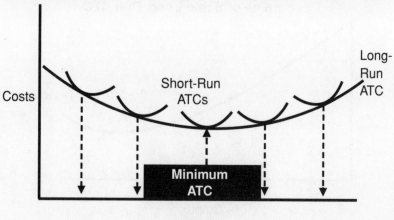

Figure 11

Industries may have differently shaped ATC curves:

- Some industries attain minimum ATC very early in production output and continue to very high output levels (figure 12).

Monopolistically Competitive Economies of Scale Long-Run ATC

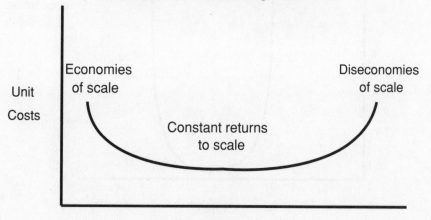

Figure 12

- Some industries do not attain minimum ATC until they reach very high levels of output (figure 13).

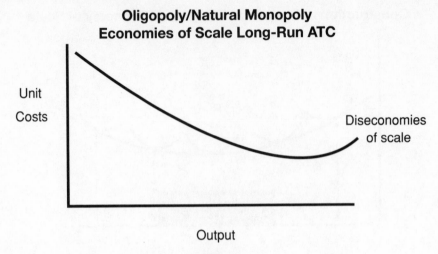

**Oligopoly/Natural Monopoly
Economies of Scale Long-Run ATC**

Figure 13

- Some industries attain minimum ATC very early in output, but also reach diseconomies of scale very quickly (figure 14).

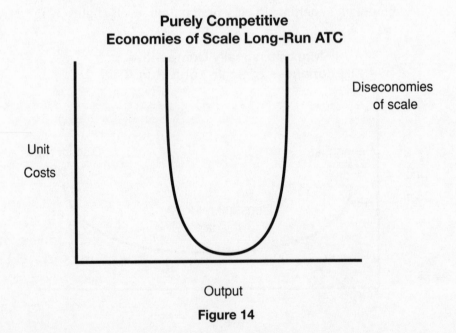

**Purely Competitive
Economies of Scale Long-Run ATC**

Figure 14

FOUR PRODUCTION MARKET MODELS

Economists group industries into four market types, based on the degree of competition present, ease of entrance or exit, and level of product standardization or differentiation. Note that the short-run cost curves of all firms are similar; what separates them is the nature of their revenue.

Profit Maximization

All four market types seek the greatest total profit possible (Total Revenue – Total Cost = profit). Firms also seek to minimize loss; as discussed earlier, they will shut down when revenue is less than minimum AVC. Profit maximization occurs when the revenue generated by one more unit of output equals the cost of that additional unit (Marginal Revenue = Marginal Cost rule), and that marginal cost is rising. This rule applies to all four market models.

Perfect Competition Market Model

The perfect competition model has four distinct characteristics:

1. Many buyers and sellers; firms are price takers, unable to influence the prices they must charge.

2. Homogenous product; each firm makes an identical product and consumers make purchases based on price comparison only.

3. Freedom of exit and entry; no barriers limit a firm's behavior.

4. Perfect information; each buyer and seller is fully informed and rational.

These assumptions allow us to draw the purely competitive firm's revenue as perfectly elastic. Although the entire market for this g/s does have a demand curve (see figure 17), we are looking at an individual firm (table 3, figure 15) within an industry. The entire industry could act together to influence price, but one firm independently could not. A single firm has no pricing power. That is why economists call firms in a perfectly competitive market "price takers." Let's revisit the table of costs we dealt with earlier and add a revenue column.

Table 3
Total, Average, and Marginal Cost Schedules in Short Run

Total Output	Total Revenue	Total Costs	Average Fixed Costs	Average Variable Costs	Average Total Costs	Marginal Costs	Marginal Revenue = Price	Total Economic Profit +Loss
Q	TR = Price × Quantity	TC = TFC+TVC	TR = TR × Quantity	$AVC = \frac{TVC}{Q}$	$ATC = \frac{TC}{Q}$	$MC = \frac{\Delta TC}{\Delta Q}$	$MR = \frac{\Delta TR}{\Delta Q}$	TR–TC = Profit
0	0	$10						−10
1	10	20	$10	$10	$20	$10	$10	−10
2	20	28	5	9	14	8	10	−8
3	30	35	3.33	8.33	11.6	7	10	−5
4	40	40	2.5	7.5	10	5	10	0
5	50	45	2	7	9	5	10	+5
6	60	52	1.66	7	8.66	7	10	+8
7	70	60.6	1.44	7.2	8.6	8.6	10	+9.4
8	80	70	1.25	7.5	8.75	9.4	10	+10
9	90	90	1.1	8.8	10	20	10	0

Profit maximization occurs at the eighth unit of output when MR = MC and MC is rising. This profit maximization point is confirmed graphically as well.

Individual Firm in Purely Competitive Market:
Short-Run Economic Profit

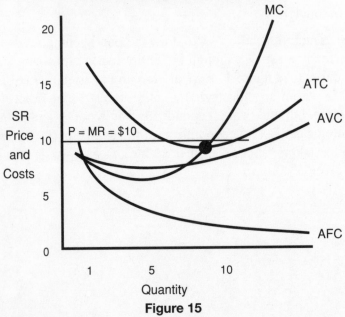

Figure 15

This firm is enjoying an economic profit, as the MR = MC is above minimum ATC. What would happen if the price fell to $8? Let's return to the table (see table 4).

Table 4
Total, Average, and Marginal Cost Schedules in Short Run

Total Output	Total Revenue	Total Costs	Average Fixed Costs	Average Variable Costs	Average Total Costs	Marginal Costs	Marginal Revenue = Price	Total Economic Profit +Loss
Q	TR = Price × Quantity	TC = TFC+TVC	TR = TR × Quantity	$AVC = \frac{TVC}{Q}$	$ATC = \frac{TC}{Q}$	$MC = \frac{\Delta TC}{\Delta Q}$	$MR = \frac{\Delta TR}{\Delta Q}$	TR–TC = Profit
0	0	$10						–10
1	8	20	$10	$10	$20	$10	$8	–12
2	16	28	5	9	14	8	8	–12
3	24	35	3.33	8.33	11.6	7	8	–11
4	34	40	2.5	7.5	10	5	8	–6
5	40	45	2	7	9	5	8	–5
6	48	52	1.66	7	8.66	7	8	–4
7	56	60.6	1.44	7.2	8.6	8.6	8	–4.6
8	64	70	1.25	7.5	8.75	9.4	8	–6
9	72	90	1.1	8.8	10	20	8	–18

The MR = MC intersection occurs at 6 units of output. The firm is losing $4 at this level, but notice that this is its minimal loss. Firms experiencing a loss will attempt to minimize loss and will not shut down as long as they are covering minimum AVC. This situation is shown in figure 16.

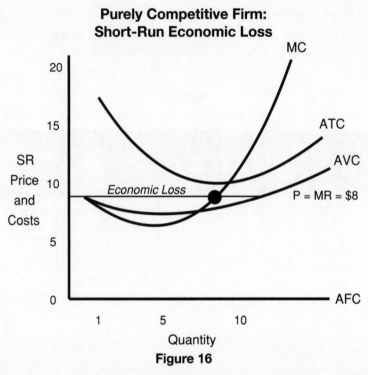

Figure 16

Individual firms believe that some firms will flee an industry because of loss, causing the industry supply curve to move up and inward. Because the industry has a downward-sloping demand curve, prices would then rise, industry output would fall, and firms would return to normal profit (which occurs at a price of $8.60, due to the fact that at 7 units of output quantity, P = D = MR = MC at minimum ATC) in the long run. This can be seen in table 5 and figure 17, which depict the supply and demand of the industry as a whole, rather than for the individual firm.

Table 5
Total, Average, and Marginal Cost Schedules in Short Run

Total Output	Total Revenue	Total Costs	Average Fixed Costs	Average Variable Costs	Average Total Costs	Marginal Costs	Marginal Revenue = Price	Total Economic Profit +Loss
Q	TR = Price × Quantity	TC = TFC+TVC	TR = TR × Quantity	$AVC = \frac{TVC}{Q}$	$ATC = \frac{TC}{Q}$	$MC = \frac{\Delta TC}{\Delta Q}$	$MR = \frac{\Delta TR}{\Delta Q}$	TR–TC = Profit
0	0	$10						−10
1	8.60	20	$10	$10	$20	$10	$8.60	−11.40
2	17.20	28	5	9	14	8	8.60	−10.80
3	25.80	35	3.33	8.33	11.6	7	8.60	−32.20
4	34.40	40	2.5	7.5	10	5	8.60	−5.60
5	43.00	45	2	7	9	5	8.60	−2.00
6	51.60	51.96	1.66	7	8.66	7	8.60	−0.36
7	60.20	60.20	1.44	7.2	8.6	8.6	8.60	0
8	68.80	70.96	1.25	7.5	8.75	9.4	8.60	−2.16
9	77.40	90	1.1	8.8	10	20	8.60	−12.60

Purely Competitive Firm and Industry:
Long-Run Normal Profit

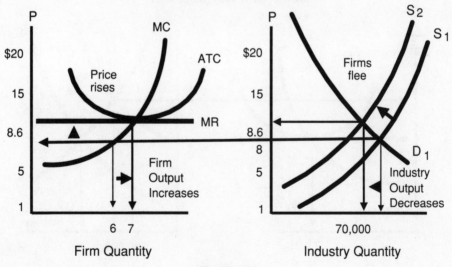

Figure 17

So too, if firms in a purely competitive market are experiencing economic profit, others will be attracted to the profit, moving the industry supply curve down and to the right. Again, because the industry has a downward-

sloping demand curve, prices will fall. This explains the long-run equilibrium concept of productive and allocative efficiency. Because firms are attracted to profit and repelled by loss, long-run equilibrium will occur at
minimum ATC. Therefore, in the long run, Price = D = MR = MC at minimum ATC and economic efficiency occurs (as shown in table 5 and figure
17). If firms are earning an economic profit, consumers are signaling the
need for greater allocation of resources to this g/s. If firms are seeing losses,
they should reduce their allocation of resources. If:

- P > MC, then resources are underallocated.

- P < MC, then resources are overallocated.

In the long run, society receives exactly what it wants, as the "invisible
hands" work. The self-interest of producers and consumer satisfaction are
maximized (productive efficiency and allocative efficiency).

What happens in the long run when the short-run price is $15? As seen
in figure 18, supply increases (S1 to S2) as more firms enter the market and
price returns to LR minimum ATC ($15.00 to $8.60). Economic profit ends
and normal profit returns to the industry.

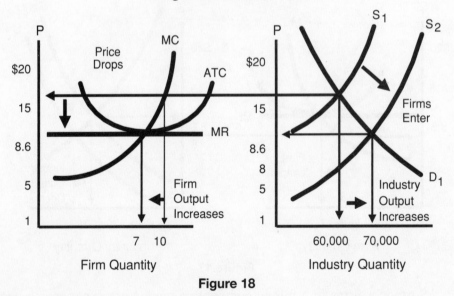

**Purely Competitive Firm and Industry:
Long-Run Normal Profit**

Figure 18

Pure Monopoly

A monopoly is an industry composed of a single firm selling a product for which there is no substitute. There are high barriers to entry into the industry, because the firm has resource control, or it may have government-granted patents and licenses. This firm has control over quantity and therefore can change price (price maker) by changing the quantity of product supplied, limited by the demand curve for the g/s. A natural monopoly occurs in industries where a declining long-run ATC curve extends over a high output quantity. This makes an individual producer more cost-efficient than several smaller firms, each producing lesser amounts. This is why economists refer to the monopolist as a "price maker." The monopolist seeks profit maximization, as all producers do. Its costs are the same, so it seeks the highest total profit, not the highest price. This is why the MR = MC rule still applies. The firm will charge the highest price possible for the level of output produced and demanded (see table 6).

Table 6
Short Run
Total and Marginal Cost, Total and Marginal Revenue Schedules

Total Output	Price Average Revenue	Total Costs	Total Revenue	Average Variable Costs	Average Total Costs	Marginal Costs	Marginal Revenue = Price	Total Economic Profit +Loss
Q	Demand	$TC = $ TFC+TVC	$TR = Price \times$ Quantity	$AVC = \dfrac{TVC}{Q}$	$ATC = \dfrac{TC}{Q}$	$MC = \dfrac{\Delta TC}{\Delta Q}$	$MR = \dfrac{\Delta TR}{\Delta Q}$	$TR{-}TC =$ Profit
0	0	$10						−10
1	22	20	$ 22	$10	$20	$10	$22	2
2	20	28	40	9	14	8	18	12
3	18	35	54	8.33	11.6	7	14	19
4	16	40	64	7.5	10	5	10	24
5	14	45	70	7	9	5	6	25
6	12	52	72	7	8.66	7	2	20
7	10	60.6	70	7.2	8.6	8.6	−2	9.4
8	8	70	64	7.5	8.75	9.4	−6	−6
9	6	90	54	8.8	10	20	−10	−36

The monopolist will produce at the output quantity of 5 units, thus operating in the elastic total revenue portion of the demand curve. Remember that in the elastic portion, an increase in output increases the total revenue.

The monopolist would not operate in the inelastic total revenue portion, as that price would result in a decrease in total revenue. As seen in table 6, any output quantity greater than 5 results in a decrease in total revenue because the consumer will not purchase that quantity (output of 6) unless the price is lowered ($12). The lower price results in a decrease in total revenue (inelastic) from $25 to $20, so the monopolist will not produce at that output level. This decision to limit production to 5 units results in maximum profitability for the firm. However, this is achieved through productive inefficiency (higher than minimum ATC) and allocative inefficiency (output below demand intersection with MC). These realities are confirmed in the model in figure 19. Note that MR = MC at a price above ATC. The shaded area represents the economic profit of the firm. If demand lessened, the monopolist could experience loss, if demand fell below ATC.

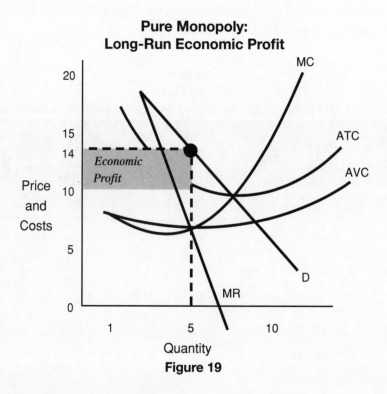

**Pure Monopoly:
Long-Run Economic Profit**

Figure 19

Monopolistic Competition

Both the purely competitive and imperfectly competitive models are extremes. Most industries and producers fall between the two. Monopolistic competition exhibits considerable competition, but with some pricing power. Pricing power comes from a firm's product quality, recognition, location, and service; in other words, from product differentiation. Firms in differentiated competition are subject to the demand curve, and so output decisions greatly affect both price and profits. It is also important to note that the demand and marginal revenue curves are more elastic for the monopolistically competitive firm than for the monopoly. The monopolistic competitor maximizes profits or minimizes loss by producing at the output level where MR = MC. Long-run economic profit is difficult, as new firms will enter just as firms will flee loss. Thus, monopolistic competitors (similar to purely competitive) earn normal profits in the long run. Also, they achieve normal profit at slightly above minimum ATC (no productive efficiency) and with output at less than allocative efficiency (similar to pure monopoly). Their situation is depicted graphically in figure 20.

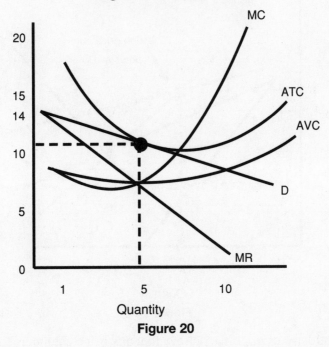

Monopolistic Competitive Firm and Industry: Long-Run Normal Profit

Figure 20

Oligopoly

An *oligopoly* is an industry dominated by a few very large firms. These firms may have either homogenous products or differentiated ones. Regardless, they are bound by mutual dependence. They are interdependent because the profitability of each firm depends on the strategies pursued by its competitors. Each firm's pricing and output strategy is determined by the expected reaction of its business rivals. It is easy to understand why a firm attempting to maximize profits would attempt to collude with its competition. This collusion could be formal (planned) or informal (unplanned). Unplanned collusion is what prevents price wars from occurring. Price wars are explained best by the kinked demand curve (figure 21). The kinked demand curve illustrates how an oligopolist will refrain from raising its price left of the kink (where demand is relatively elastic). This would lower market share and total revenue for the oligopolist firm, as its competitors would not follow a price increase. However, if an oligopolist lowered its price right of the kink (where demand is relatively inelastic), it would not gain market share, because its competitors would tend to follow the price decrease.

Oligopoly:
Kinked Demand Curve

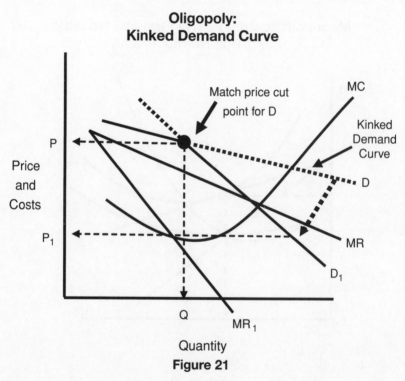

Figure 21

Noncollusive oligopolies believe that any price change is for the worse (raise price, lose customers/lower price, lose revenue), so they seek stable prices. Often a firm that begins incurring higher costs will attempt or announce an intended price hike ("price leader") and then respond to its rivals' behavior. In some situations, when a rival is in a weakened condition (carrying a high debt load, for example), a firm may engage in a price war to force the rival out of business or into a merger. Economist's employ a concept known as "game theory" to study behavior associated with the interdependence present in oligopolies. Game theory explores the realization by oligopolists that their profit is as dependent upon the action/reaction of their competitor (assume a duopoly – 2 producers) as its own. Analysis of the nature and degree of interdependence present in an oligopoly leads to various strategic behaviors by firms. The relationship type shown below is typical of firms that are competitively balanced. The various payoffs possible for firms can be viewed in a simple game cube or matrix as shown in figure 22.

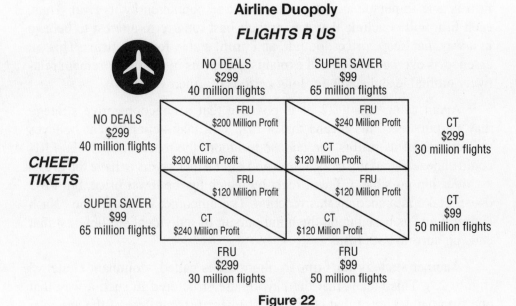

Figure 22

Notice that:

1. If Flights R Us (FRU) pursues a "no deal" strategy and Cheep Tikets (CT) matches the "no deal" policy, a price of $299 results with 40 million flights each and a common profit of $200 million results.

2. If FRU pursues a super saver strategy and CT fails to lower its prices the increase in ridership, 40 to 65 million flights, would result in FRU profits increasing while CT suffers a loss of ridership, 40 to 30 million flights, and profits decrease to $120 million.

3. If CT pursues a super saver strategy and FRU fails to lower its prices the increase in ridership, 40 to 65 million, would result in CT profits increasing to $240 million, while FRU suffers a loss of ridership, 40 to 30 million flights, and profits decrease to $120 million.

4. If FRU pursues a super saver strategy and CT matches the "super saver" both see an increase in flights, 40 million to 50 million, with a reduction in profits to $120 million.

It is easy to understand why firms in oligopoly hesitate to change prices. A lowering of price may result in a price war where both producers see a decline in profits. These outcomes result from neither firm having an advantage in pursuing either low price strategy. Economists will refer to this behavior strategy as "tit for tat." It is clear from the payoff matrix that neither firm is able to pursue a strategy that can't be countered by its rival. Thus, each firm will conclude that it is in their best long-term interest to behave in a way that keeps prices, output, and profit stable for both firms. This, in essence, is overt collusion and explains why firms in oligopoly remain relatively profitable and stable for long periods of time.

Again using figure 22, it is possible that a noncooperative strategy may be pursued. This means that a firm will take action that it believes will maximize its profits and choose to ignore the reaction of rivals. FRU could choose to maximize its output and offer super savers to have the greatest ridership possible. CT will react by matching the lower price, but FRU doesn't take into account this reaction. The outcome, known as the "Nash equilibrium," is based upon the blind pursuit of individual self-interest that ends up hurting both firms.

Another strategy for firms in oligopoly is called "dominant strategy" (figure 23). This means that the payoffs are structured in such a way that one firm had a choice that is in its best interest, regardless of the action if its competitor.

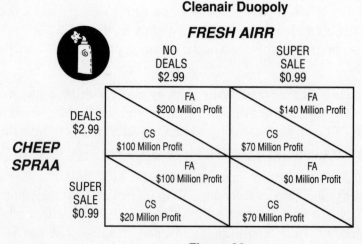

Cleanair Duopoly

FRESH AIRR

		NO DEALS $2.99	SUPER SALE $0.99
CHEEP SPRAA	DEALS $2.99	FA $200 Million Profit / CS $100 Million Profit	FA $140 Million Profit / CS $70 Million Profit
	SUPER SALE $0.99	FA $100 Million Profit / CS $20 Million Profit	FA $0 Million Profit / CS $70 Million Profit

Figure 23

FRESH AIRR (FA) has a dominant strategy whereas CHEEP SPRAA (CS) does not. CS's decision-making is dependent on FA strategy. It is in a reactive environment. There is no single pricing structure that would allow CS to raise its profits at the expense of FA. On the other hand, FA should clearly pursue a high-priced strategy of $2.99. It is clearly the highest profit selection for the firm and it doesn't depend on any reaction by CS. CHEEP SPRAA does not have a dominant strategy.

Cartels

It is easy to understand why firms would be willing to act together to avoid price wars. When acting as one, they in essence are a monopoly. Price can be dictated through output limits. This behavior is illegal in the United States and therefore would have to be undertaken secretly to fix prices. OPEC is the best example of an ongoing cartel; this group of 11 major oil producers, led by Saudi Arabia, attempts to control oil prices through overt agreement on each producer's output quota. At times, such as in 1974, 1978, and in mid-2000, output cutbacks by OPEC caused prices to rise sharply. These higher oil prices have been difficult for OPEC to maintain in the long run, however. There are obstacles to the success of cartels, such as members having different production efficiencies, higher prices attracting new firms, substitutes being developed, conflict between members, members secretly cheating, or the consumer's economy slumping into recession because of the higher costs being forced upon it.

FACTOR MARKETS

In this section of the course, students learn that the concepts of supply and demand apply to markets for factors such as land, labor, and capital, as well as to product markets. Students analyze the concept of derived demand, examine the relationship of the demand for a factor to the factor's marginal product, and consider the role of factor prices in the allocation of scarce resources. When the markets for different factors are considered separately, students generally give most attention to the labor market, particularly labor supply, and wage and employment determination. Although the course may emphasize perfectly competitive labor markets, the effect of deviations from perfect competition, such as minimum wages, unions, and product market monopolies, can be considered. For the factors of land and capital, students might examine the concept of economic rent and the relationship of the interest rate to the supply and demand for investment funds. By studying the determination of factor prices, students gain an understanding of the sources of income inequality in a market economy.

PRICING AND EMPLOYMENT OF FACTOR MARKETS

Remember the importance of the factor (resource) market in the circular flow of g/s in a free market economy. Firms purchase their input factors (land, labor, capital, and entrepreneurial management) from households. To predict the pricing of inputs, we have to examine the nature of the demand and supply for those inputs.

MARGINAL RESOURCE PRODUCTIVITY THEORY

Marginal resource productivity theory is built upon the premise that supply of and demand for inputs is purely competitive. To a producer, the demand for resource inputs is a derived demand. The value of the resource input is determined by the demand for the g/s that the input is used to produce. Therefore, the demand for an input will depend on:

- The productivity of the input in creating the finished g/s.

- The price of the finished g/s that has been produced by the resource input.

For the sake of simplicity, let's use the resource input of labor for this review. A producer would record the increasing units of labor and the resultant change in total output. This allows us to calculate the marginal product. Assuming that the market price of the finished good remains constant, we can also calculate the total revenue at each level of output and thus the marginal revenue product (MRP). The formula is:

$$MRP = \frac{\text{change in TR}}{\text{unit change in resource quantity}}$$

If we also calculate the amount that each additional unit of labor input adds to the producer's total cost, we get its marginal resource cost (MRC). The formula is:

$$MRC = \frac{\text{change in total input cost}}{\text{unit change in input quantity}}$$

A firm would use the profit-maximizing strategy of hiring one more worker, as long as the worker's contribution to revenue exceeded the increased cost to the firm (MRP = MRC). This can be viewed in table 7.

Table 7

Units of Resource Labor Inputs	Total Product Output	Marginal Product	Product Price	Total Revenue	Marginal Revenue Product	Marginal Resource Cost (assume each employee receives same wage of $125)
1	6	6	$100	$600	$600	$125
2	19	13	100	1,900	1,300	125
3	25	6	100	2,500	600	125
4	29	4	100	2,900	400	125
5	31	2	100	3,100	200	125
6	32	1	100	3,200	100	125
7	32	0	100	3,200	0	125

This firm would hire 5 units of resource labor inputs, because the fifth employee contributes more revenue ($200) than he adds in cost ($125). If a sixth employee were added, her contribution to revenue ($100) would be less than her added cost ($125), thereby decreasing the firm's profit.

Our analyses of a producer's behavior become more complicated in the real world, as neither product prices nor resource costs are purely competitive. As shown in table 8, not only do product prices decrease as more units are sold, but labor prices also increase as more workers are hired. Nonetheless, the firm would still operate at the profit-maximizing level where MRP ≥ MRC. In this case, 4 units of labor would be employed.

Table 8

Units of Resource Labor Inputs	Total Product Output	Marginal Product	Product Price	Total Revenue	Marginal Revenue Product	Total Labor Cost _assume with each added employee wage costs increase by $10_	Marginal Resource Cost
1	6	6	$280	$1680	$1,680	(60) 60	$60
2	19	13	260	4,940	3,260	(70) 140	80
3	25	6	240	6,000	1,060	(80) 240	100
4	29	4	220	6,380	380	(90) 360	120
5	31	2	200	6,200	−180	(100) 500	140
6	32	1	185	5,920	−280	(110) 660	160
7	32	0	185	5,920	0	(120) 840	180

At this point, we need to consider the reality that resources are combined in production. For example, how do firms balance the inputs of capital with labor inputs to minimize costs? Firms will seek a least-cost combination of resources that will produce an equal marginal product with the last dollar expended on each resource. In other words:

$$\frac{\text{Marginal Product of Labor (MP}_\text{L})}{\text{Price of Labor (P}_\text{L})} = \frac{\text{Marginal Product of Capital (MP}_\text{C})}{\text{Price of Capital (P}_\text{C})}$$

If the MP_L was 6 and the MP_C was 3, and each had a price of $1, what should a firm do?

Since $\frac{6}{1} > \frac{3}{1}$, the firm should spend less on capital and more on labor.

If it spent nothing on capital, the firm would lose 3 units. It would recapture those lost units by spending $0.50 more on labor, yielding a cost savings of $0.50 to the firm.

To determine the profit-maximizing combination of two factors of production, a firm must employ each resource (factor) to the point that its marginal revenue product equals its price. Using the formula,

$$\frac{\text{MRP}_\text{L}}{\text{P}_\text{L}} = \frac{\text{MRP}_\text{C}}{\text{P}_\text{C}} = 1,$$

the profit-maximizing blend could be achieved. Note that when applying the profit-maximizing equation, a firm is also employing the least-cost combination. However, the reverse is not necessarily the case. A firm operating at least-cost with multiple factors may not be operating at profit-maximizing output levels. Again, a table can be used to demonstrate the formula at work (table 9).

Table 9

Units of Resource Labor Inputs	Total Product Output	Marginal Product	Total Revenue ($2)	MRP$_L$ Price of $4	Total Product Output	Marginal Product	Total Revenue ($2)	Marginal Price of $12
1	6	6	13	13	13	13	$26	$26
2	19	13	38	25	22	9	44	18
3	25	6	50	22	28	6	56	12
4	29	4	58	8	32	4	64	8
5	31	2	62	4	35	3	70	6
6	32	1	64	2	37	2	74	4
7	32	0	64	0	38	1	76	2

Least-cost profit maximizing would occur for the firm when it combines 5 units of labor with 3 units of capital. In algebraic form,

$$\frac{MRP_L 4}{\$4} = \frac{MRP_C 12}{\$12} = 1.$$

Let's compare this X combination of 5 units of labor (producing 31 units with revenue of $62) and (5 × $4 =) $20 cost with 3 capital (producing 28 units with revenue of $56) and (3 × $12 =) $36 cost to another combination, Y. The X blend has a TR of $118 minus a TC of $56 and a profit of $62.

The Y combination of 3 units of labor (producing 25 units with revenue of $50) and (3 × $4 =) $12 cost with 3 capital (producing 28 units with revenue of $56) and (3 × $12 =) $36 cost. The Y combination has a TR of $106 minus a TC of $48 and a lesser profit of $58. The X combination is the least-cost, maximum-profit combination of resource inputs.

THE LABOR MARKET AND WAGES

Most Americans are concerned about the labor market in general, particularly labor supply and wage and employment determination. Your wage determines your standard of living. The first important distinction regarding income is the difference between nominal (dollar amount of wage) and real wages (quantity of g/s your wage purchases). With this in mind, it is easy to see the direct relationship between increased productivity, real wages, and rising standards of living. By applying the previous concepts of determination of factor prices (derived demand), an economist explains the sources of income inequality in a market economy. Some workers compete in perfectly competitive labor markets. Others experience the effect of deviations from perfect competition, such as minimum wage laws, the union effect, and monopsony.

Purely Competitive Labor Market

In a purely competitive market, the laws of supply and demand are at work (remember that the demand for labor is the MRP of labor), and they determine the wage rate and quantity of workers hired in an industry. The industry wage rate would be determined by supply and demand but vewed as perfectly elastic by the individual firm and therefore determine its MRC. So, for example, if the industry demand (MRP) for labor increased, the wage paid and the number of workers hired within an industry would also increase (figure 24).

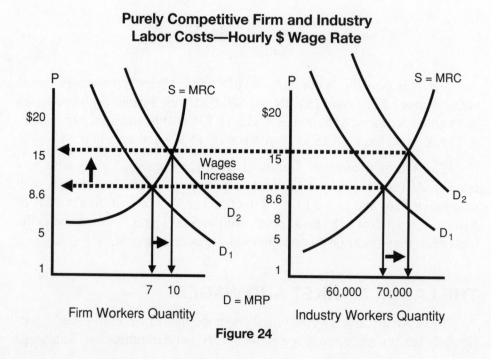

Purely Competitive Firm and Industry Labor Costs—Hourly $ Wage Rate

Figure 24

Monopsony

Monopsony is a market situation in which there is just one buyer of a resource input. A monopsonistic firm hires an additional unit of labor as long as its MRC = MRP. A monopsonist has an upward-sloping supply curve of labor. This means that to hire an additional unit of labor, it must pay that worker a higher wage. When the monopsonist pays the new worker the higher wage, it must also pay that wage to all the workers it currently employs (because current workers would be extremely dissatisfied if a new worker outearned them). This means that the MRC of the new worker is equal to the new worker's wage added to the amount necessary to bring all current workers to that new wage as well. This is important because now the MRC curve lies above the supply of workers, unlike the purely competitive market where supply equaled MRC. Therefore, the least-cost, profit-maximizing formula previously stated will apply: namely, MRC = MRP = 1. The monopsonist maximizes profits by both hiring and paying labor at its MRC = MRP wage rate and quantity, not the supply equilibrium rate or quantity. In other words, the monopsonist underhires and underpays market price and quantity of labor. Figure 25 demonstrates this concept.

Monopsonist Labor Market

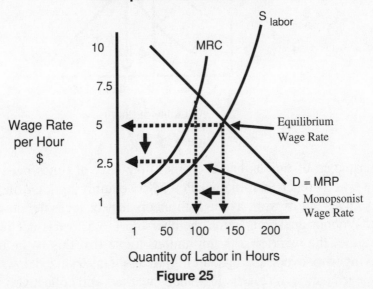

Quantity of Labor in Hours

Figure 25

Notice that the monopsonist hires the quantity of resource labor, 100 workers, and pays the lower rate of $2.50 (MRP = MRC), rather than the 150 workers at $5.00-per-hour wage equilibrium for a purely competitive market firm. The monopsonistic firm is looking to maximize profits by paying labor less than its MRP.

Union Effect

Unions affect the labor market in several ways, but perhaps the foremost is by limiting the supply of labor that a firm can draw upon. This restriction of labor supply (S to S_1) can extract a higher wage at the MRP = MRC equilibrium. This higher wage comes at the price of jobs, in that the higher cost causes a firm to hire fewer workers than it would in a nonunion market. Figure 26 illustrates this situation.

Unionized Labor Market

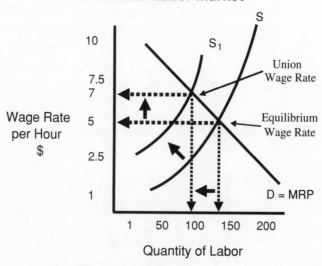

Figure 26

A criticism of unions has been that they have at times been able to extract a wage higher than the MRP = MRC equilibrium, and in essence put themselves out of work as the firm incurs loss or faces nonunion competition. Without question, union membership (13.5%) has declined as a percentage of the workforce. Many unions argue that this is the result of firms taking work overseas (outsourcing) to less industrialized, lower-wage, nonunionized nations. Nevertheless, many workers still collectively bargain their wages and benefits. All workers are protected by the Civil Rights Act as well as federal labor laws and the National Labor Relations Board (NLRB) investigates reports of abuse of workers.

EFFICIENCY, EQUITY, AND THE ROLE OF GOVERNMENT

It is important for students to understand the arguments for and against government intervention in an otherwise competitive market. Students examine the conditions for economic efficiency and the ways in which public goods and externalities generate market failures even in perfectly competitive economies. In addition, students are expected to study the effectiveness of government policies designed to correct market failures such as subsidies, taxes, quantity controls, and public provision of goods and services. Although there is not a generally accepted standard for judging the equity of an economy's income distribution, a well-designed course will examine the impact of government tax policies and transfer programs on the distribution of income and on economic efficiency.

GOVERNMENT INTERVENTION

In addition to the intervention already reviewed, other shortcomings in the free market system may be addressed by further government action. These shortcomings are dealt with through public goods, production standards, and regulation of business practices.

Market Failure

The free market system is considered to experience failure when it does not efficiently organize the means of production or allocate goods and services to consumers. Furthermore, it is contended that a nonprofit public institution would be more efficient and broadly beneficial than a private alternative. The two main areas of market failure are found when

1. costs or benefits not borne by the market participants occur

2. goods and services are not subject to division or exclusion

These shortcomings are dealt with through creation of public goods, regulated production standards and business practices.

Public Goods

Certain goods and services are difficult or impossible to deliver through the free market, as there is no profit incentive for private production thereof.

Adam Smith recognized this, and mentioned defense, roads, education, and medical care as being among them. Public goods are neither divisible nor exclusionary (there is shared consumption and nonexclusion). It would be difficult to charge on an individual basis for law enforcement, courts, airports, or fighter planes. Therefore, goods that provide for the common good fall into this category. Disagreement over the nature and extent of these g/s is present today. Some argue that public goods such as education are not best delivered by government, but rather should be held to federal standards and privatized through a voucher system.

Negative and Positive Externalities

Economists describe (spillover) costs or (spillover) benefits that are borne by parties not directly associated with an economic activity in the marketplace as *externalities*. An example of a spillover benefit is public flu shots. Even though you may not receive a shot, your exposure is diminished as a result, and you will not have to help pay the hospital costs for those who would have gotten sick. A spillover cost is the pollution that results from production of a good that spews sulfur into the air. There is no direct cost. Government can tax the polluter to cover the cost of clean air, or even require prevention of the pollution in the first place, through environmental standards. Many government taxes and subsidies are employed to encourage or discourage economic activities with externalities.

Government Industrial Regulation

Government at the end of the nineteenth century concluded that some individuals had created companies that monopolized market forces in a way that was detrimental to society. Therefore, a series of antitrust laws (Sherman, 1890; Clayton, 1914; Federal Trade Commission Act, 1914; and the Celler-Kefauver Act, 1950) were passed that together provide the legal basis for government regulation of business. The FTC and the Justice Department each help protect the degree of competition necessary for the free market to operate efficiently. We have already reviewed the natural tendency of firms to seek merger in order to maximize profits. Government can act to prevent mergers or to break up firms that violate acceptable levels of competition. In the 1980s, much relaxation of enforcement resulted in deregulation of some firms (airlines, utilities) and allowed increased concentration in others (food and beverage).

Merger Types

There are three basic types of merger: horizontal, merging two similar producers; vertical, merging two firms that are part of a goods production process; and conglomerate, merging different industries or multinational companies. Firms seeking mergers of this latter nature must seek government approval prior to conclusion of any agreement. If denied, they may appeal through the court system. This has become increasingly complicated, as the United States may approve a merger only to have it denied by the European Union (as with the proposed GE and Honeywell merger), and vice versa.

MAIN GOVERNMENT INTERVENTION METHODS

If the general public, lobbyists, and government conclude that a g/s is over/underpriced or over/undersupplied, the government may alter the market structure to encourage or discourage price and quantity changes. This can be accomplished through either a price ceiling or a price floor. In addition to altering free market delivery of goods and services, government also alters income distribution through taxation structure as well as targeted spending programs. The burden of taxation and government spending programs are heatedly debated. This review cannot address these issues in depth but you should be aware that they exist and will be of significance in your life.

Price Ceiling

A government price ceiling is a declaration that the price charged by suppliers is too high. Therefore, the government legislates a price cap. Producers cannot by law charge a price higher than that set by government. This maximum price may appear attractive to consumers if it applies to items like rent or food staples, like sugar during wartime. A supply and demand model helps to illustrate the issue. Let's use rent control for a one-bedroom apartment as an example.

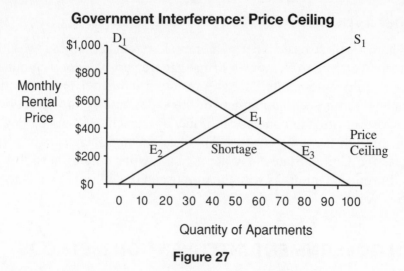

Figure 27

The government price ceiling depicted in figure 27 shows the effect that a cap on price has on the marketplace. Equilibrium price for the apartment would be $300 and equilibrium supply is 40,000 units. The government then mandates a rent control ceiling of $100 to landlords. This new forced price will cause a swelling of demand for these apartments to 60,000 units. However, landlords will supply only 20,000 units at this price. Where do the apartment units go? If profit is not present, firms will flee the market. Perhaps they convert the apartments into condominiums or office space, which are markets free from government control. Many other negative externalities may occur, such as the formation of a black market, poor quality of remaining apartments, higher prices for similar goods, and diversion of investment from housing.

Price Floors

A government price floor is a declaration that the price paid by consumers is too low. This results in production levels that may deprive some consumers of the g/s. Therefore, the government legislates a price minimum. This new price minimum, set above equilibrium, will stimulate production, as new profit levels are guaranteed to producers. Consumers cannot by law pay a price lower than that set by the government. This higher minimum price (especially for items such as food staples) is often justified by the realization of other societal benefits, such as maintenance of family farm ownership. If government intervention is predicated on a socioeconomic premise that overproduction of this g/s has spillover benefits, higher prices or subsidy of production are supported. A supply and demand model helps to illustrate the issue. Let's use milk production as an example (figure 28).

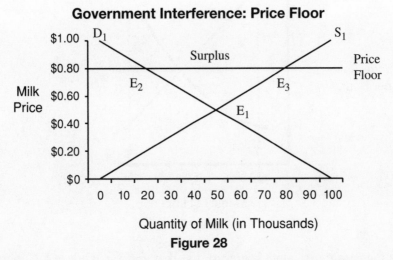

Figure 28

Assume that the free-market price for milk is $0.50 per quart and that 50,000 quarts are purchased each day. Government supports a new minimum price of $0.80 for producers. This new, higher price will stimulate suppliers to supply 80,000 quarts of milk daily. However, the higher price also causes the quantity demanded by consumers to fall to 20,000 quarts. This new minimum price results in a surplus of 60,000 quarts of milk. The dilemma now facing the government is how to dispose of the surplus milk. Should the good be transferred to the poor? Should it be destroyed? Should the government simply pay for nonproduction? The new, higher price disrupts the rationing effect of the free market. Allocative and productive efficiency are destroyed. For this reason, most economists generally oppose government interference in free markets.

Minimum Wage Laws

Government intervention into the purely competitive market for labor would act much the same as our earlier model of rent controls. If minimum wage were set above equilibrium ($10), firms would hire fewer workers (25) and the workers seeking those jobs (125) would be numerous. Conversely, if minimum wage were below equilibrium, firms would seek to pay down to the legal wage, but few workers would be interested in working at that price. This can be viewed graphically in figure 29.

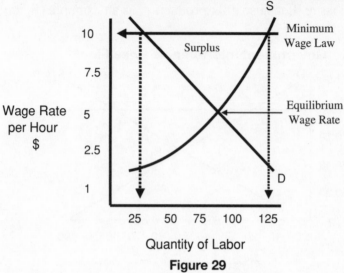

Minimum Wage Law Above Market Equilibrium

Figure 29

In the minimum wage scenario, the demand for labor at $10 per hour would be very low, whereas the number of job seekers would be extremely high. This minimum wage would result in a surplus of labor. This is one of the main arguments against minimum wage.

Proponents counter this argument by pointing out that, in the real world, the affected low-pay labor market is subject to some monopsony power. As shown in figure 30, the monopsonist firm would hire 150 hours of labor and

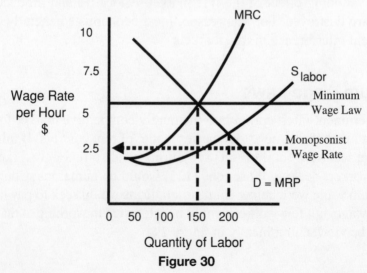

Minimum Wage Law (Some Monopsony)

Figure 30

pay workers $5 per hour (MRC), even though they generate $10 in revenue (MRP), and thus create economic profit. The wage could be increased to $10 without causing unemployment, as the firm could afford to pay $10 and still make a normal profit.

INCOME INEQUALITY AND POVERTY

Advocates of government wage intervention suggest that the income disparity resulting from the free market is too great. The debate over how much disparity between rich and poor should be allowed to exist is ongoing (refer to fiscal policy review). Furthermore, there is additional heated argument over what method to use to address this inequity issue, and to what extent. The most widely used measure to demonstrate income distribution over time is the Lorenz curve, shown in figure 31. The Lorenz curve contrasts five equal percentile groupings of population with their percentage share of total income. The income used is before tax and includes cash transfer payments; it does not include noncash transfers (food stamps, Medicaid, etc.). A bisection of the graph provides a perfectly direct relationship between population and income of that population. Therefore, the greater the actual distribution curve bows outward from the diagonal line, the greater the degree of income inequality.

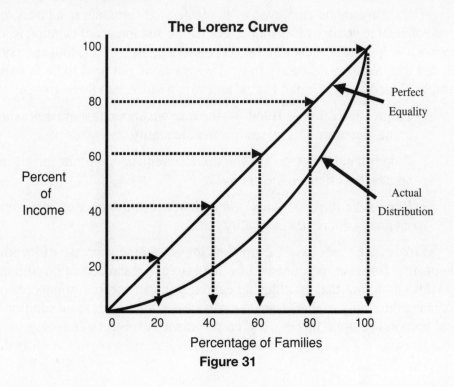

Figure 31

U.S. income distribution is significantly more equal than the Lorenz curve for the world as a whole. Proponents of increased government intervention for more even distribution of income advocate increased progressive income taxes, transfer payments, aid to education, and laws designed to end discrimination. Critics of this analysis believe that several flaws are present in this contention, including:

- Arbitrary income limits for income categories.

- Time frame fails to account for changes in earnings over lifetime.

- Income is nominal and does not account for an overall rise in the standard of living. (It measures your percentage piece of the pie, not the overall size of the pie, which might have increased.)

- Income does not measure changes in other assets that constitute wealth.

- Higher incomes reflect behaviors that result in high productivity. Remove the resulting income, and the incentive to exhibit those characteristics fades, along with growth in productivity.

TAXATION

The main method employed by the Federal government to address the issue of income disparity is taxation. The nature and impact of taxation is, of course, controversial. Adam Smith addressed the issue of taxation and concluded that taxes are necessary to fund government, but need to be fair and simple. Sounds easy! United States' taxes are divided into three groups;

- Progressive ("Robin Hood")—the marginal tax rate increases as income increases. Decreases income inequality.

- Proportional ("flat tax")—the tax rate remains constant for all incomes. No effect on inequality.

- Regressive (e.g., sales tax)—marginal tax rate decreases as income increases. Increases inequality.

Progressive taxes have the greatest impact on the decrease of income inequality. However, proponents of a flat tax (or greater reduction of marginality) point out that by reducing capital in upper income groups one is reducing the ability of that group to grow the economy and create additional real economic output, income, and employment. A subject of ongoing societal debate is the issue of whether the higher income group's wealth is the result of their creation of economic growth or a reduction in the income of the lower income group.

Taxation and Loss of Economic Efficiency

Oftentimes government chooses to address negative externalities, such as pollution, with the imposition of a tax upon the offending good or service. Even though the government may seek fairness in the assessment of tax, the result is a tradeoff between efficiency and equity. When a tax is imposed, a wedge is driven between the consumer and producer that distorts the market and results in loss of efficiency in both consumption and production as we move away from equilibrium. In other words, consumers pay more for less and producers provide less at reduced price/revenue. Furthermore, depending upon elasticities the burden of the loss may not be shared equally (perceived fairness). For example, if the demand for the good or service is highly price inelastic, producers can shift a greater portion of the tax to the consumer (as in tobacco and alcohol sales). Finally, recall the topic of consumer and producer surplus (combined to create total societal satisfaction). The imposition of a tax causes a deadweight loss (efficiency reduced with a decrease in total societal satisfaction), as shown in figure 32. The shift from

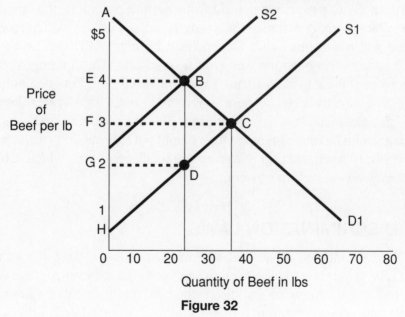

Consumer, Producer Surplus & Deadweight Loss

Figure 32

S1 to S2 would be equal to the tax levy. The tax creates a gap between the price received by producers G2 and the price paid by consumers E4. As a result of the after tax prices the quantity bought and sold falls from 50 to 30 units. At point B, if there were no tax, the marginal benefit of 20 additional units is greater than the marginal cost of that production. Thus, due to the tax, society loses the potential gain in total satisfaction from the production and consumption of the higher level of output. This deadweight loss is measured by area B – C – D. This "loss" represents the excess burden placed on society above the tax revenue collected, represented by areas G2, E4, B, and D. If the intent of government is to affect a change in societal behavior, taxes can be an effective incentive. Finally, don't forget that a bureaucracy (additional cost) is created to process taxes as well as the time loss involved in filing the required forms.

TRANSFER PAYMENTS

In conjunction with the impact unequal taxation has upon origin of government revenues is the spending destination of those monies, as it further addresses income inequality. The main transfer programs are social insurance programs (Medicaid, Medicare, Social Security, SSI, food stamps, Housing Assistance, and TANF) guaranteed to all citizens who qualify. They are entitled to the benefits of these programs by law. Many people qualify because of a disability, illness, unemployment, or other specified misfortune. Other people receive aid from welfare programs, the largest of which is Temporary Assistance for Needy Families (TANF), which recently replaced Aid to Families with Dependent Children (AFDC). The cost of these programs has been increasing at a rapid rate. The funding of these programs continues to be a major source of discussion between political parties. The effectiveness of these programs in reducing poverty depends on the measurement criteria. Some argue that without assistance, human suffering would be much greater. Others point out that public assistance is a disincentive to work and improve one's economic condition, which leads to dependency on the welfare system.

ANTIDISCRIMINATION LAWS

Disparate income for women and minorities is a matter of historical record. The government has several means by which it can encourage equal employment opportunity to end discrimination: maintain full employment, improve educational or training opportunities, and mandate practices that assist statistical equality. Beginning in 1963 with the Equal Pay Act, and continuing with Title VII of the 1964 Civil Rights Act, and affirmative action required by Executive Orders of 1965 and 1968, proponents believe much good has been done in addressing unequal opportunity in America. Some argue that more should be done in the future. Opponents, of affirmative action in particular, point out that this preferential treatment is reverse discrimination. A series of federal and Supreme Court cases upheld the constitutionality of affirmative action in 1986 and 1987, but reignited the debate in 1995 when the Supreme Court ruled that public universities may not justify quotas based on the benefits of diversity. Some states, such as California and Washington, have amended their laws to end gender or racial preferences.

PRACTICE TEST 1

This test is also on CD-ROM in our special interactive TEST*ware*® for the CLEP Principles of Microeconomics exam. It is highly recommended that you first take this exam on computer. You will then have the additional study features and benefits of enforced time conditions, individual diagnostic analysis, and instant scoring.

CLEP Microeconomics

PRACTICE TEST 1

TIME: 90 Minutes
80 Questions

(Answer sheets appear in the back of this book.)

DIRECTIONS: Each of the questions or incomplete statements below is followed by five suggested answers or completions. Select the best answer for each question and then fill in the corresponding oval on the answer sheet.

---

1. The primary focus of microeconomics is

    (A) the aggregate supply and aggregate demand resultant output

    (B) unlimited resources and unlimited wants

    (C) the specific economic components that make up the economic system

    (D) concealment of detailed information about specific segments of the economy

    (E) manipulating overall performance of the economic system

2. Economic efficiency is mainly concerned with

    (A) the limited wants–unlimited resources dilemma

    (B) considerations of equity in the distribution of wealth

    (C) obtaining the maximum output from available resources

    (D) creating the greatest societal satisfaction from resources

    (E) the transfer of wealth in an equitable fashion

3. A production possibilities curve is "bowed out" from the origin because

  (A) input resources are not equally efficient in producing two alternative goods

  (B) Keynes recognized this reality and modern economists follow his theory

  (C) specialization of output increases input potential

  (D) resources are scarce

  (E) wants are virtually unlimited

4. Opportunity cost

  (A) is reflected in the convex curve of cost models

  (B) does not apply to socialistic economies, because of central planning

  (C) suggests that the use of resources in any particular line of production means that alternative outputs must be forgone

  (D) is irrelevant if the production possibilities curve is shifting to the right

  (E) suggests that insatiable wants can be fulfilled

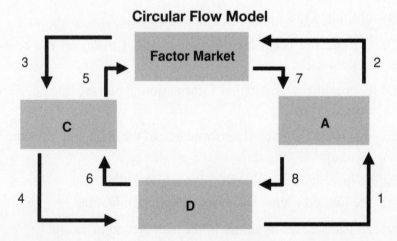

Circular Flow Model

5. In the preceding circular flow model of a free market economy, flow (4) represents

  (A) wage, rent, interest, and profit income

  (B) land, labor, capital, and entrepreneurial ability

(C) goods and services brought to the product market

(D) consumer expenditures

(E) costs of production

6. "As the retail price of a good increases, consumers shift their purchases to other products whose prices are now relatively lower." This statement describes

(A) an inferior good

(B) the rationing function of prices

(C) the substitution effect

(D) opportunity cost

(E) the income effect

7. If the demand curve for product B shifts to the right as the price of product A declines, it can be concluded that

(A) A and B are both inferior goods

(B) A is a superior good and B is an inferior good

(C) A is an inferior good and B is a superior good

(D) A and B are complementary goods

(E) A and B are substitute goods

8. Assume that the demand schedule for concrete is downward sloping. If the price of concrete falls from $2.50 to $2.00 a pound

(A) the quantity demanded of concrete will decrease

(B) the demand for concrete will decrease

(C) the quantity demanded of concrete will increase

(D) the demand for concrete will increase

(E) the demand for concrete will shift to the left

9. Assume that a drought in Kansas reduces the supply of barley. Barley is a basic ingredient in the production of beer, and wine is a consumer substitute for beer. Therefore, we would expect the price of beer to

   (A) rise, the supply of beer to increase, and the demand for wine to increase

   (B) rise, the supply of beer to decrease, and the demand for wine to increase

   (C) rise, the supply of beer to decrease, and the demand for wine to decrease

   (D) fall, the supply of beer to increase, and the demand for wine to increase

   (E) remain the same, the supply of beer to remain constant, and the demand will be unchanged

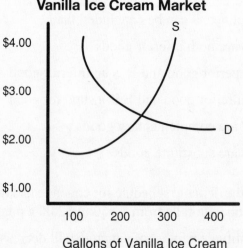

Vanilla Ice Cream Market

Gallons of Vanilla Ice Cream

10. Refer to the preceding diagram. The equilibrium price and quantity in the vanilla ice cream market will be approximately

    (A) $1.00 and 200

    (B) $1.60 and 130

    (C) $0.50 and 130

    (D) $1.60 and 290

    (E) $2.50 and 250

11. Specialization in production is desirable because it

    (A) allows everyone to have a job that he or she likes

    (B) permits the production of a larger output with fixed amounts of resources

    (C) facilitates trade by bartering

    (D) increases output of goods at higher prices

    (E) guarantees full employment

Answer **Question 12** on the basis of the following information.

Suppose 30 units of product A can be produced by employing just labor and capital in the 4 ways shown below. Assume that the prices of labor and capital are $2 and $3 respectively.

Production techniques possible combinations:

	I	II	III	IV
Labor	4	3	2	5
Capital	2	3	5	1

12. Assuming that the price of product A is $0.50 and that all 30 units will be sold, the firm will realize

    (A) an economic profit of $4

    (B) an economic profit of $2

    (C) an economic profit of $6

    (D) a loss of $6

    (E) a loss of $3

13. Assume that a normal good is being produced in a competitive industry that is in long-run equilibrium. If average consumer income increased, which of the following combinations would result?

Output	Price	# of firms in industry
(A) Decrease	Decrease	Exit
(B) Decrease	Decrease	Enter
(C) Increase	Decrease	Exit
(D) Decrease	Increase	Exit
(E) Increase	Increase	Enter

14. The free market system does not produce public goods because

I. There is inadequate demand for such goods.

II. People who do not pay for the goods cannot be prevented from consuming them.

III. Collecting revenue from production of such goods is difficult.

(A) I only

(B) II only

(C) III only

(D) Both I and III

(E) Both II and III

15. The price of product X is reduced from $100 to $90. As a result, the quantity demanded increases from 50 to 60 units. Therefore, demand for X in this price elasticity range

(A) has declined

(B) is of unit elasticity

(C) is inelastic

(D) results in lower total revenue for firms

(E) is elastic

16. Suppose that a 20 percent increase in the price of normal good Y causes a 10 percent decline in the quantity demanded of normal good X. The coefficient of cross elasticity of demand is

    (A) negative, and therefore these goods are substitutes

    (B) negative, and thus income sensitive

    (C) negative, and therefore these goods are complements

    (D) positive, and therefore these goods are substitutes

    (E) positive, and therefore these goods are complements

17. Assume that a 3 percent increase in income in the economy produces a 1 percent decline in the quantity demanded of good X. The outcome would be

Coefficient of Income Elasticity	Type of Good X is:
(A) negative	inferior good
(B) negative	normal good
(C) positive	inferior good
(D) positive	normal good
(E) negative	unrelated

18. The first sport drink yields Craig 18 units of utility and the second yields him an additional 12 units of utility. His total utility from three sport drinks is 36 units of utility. The marginal utility of the third sport drink is

    (A) 26 units of utility

    (B) 6 units of utility

    (C) 8 units of utility

    (D) 54 total utils

    (E) 38 total utils

Answer **Questions 19 and 20** on the basis of the following table, which shows the amounts of additional satisfaction (marginal utility) that a consumer derives from successive quantities of products X and Y.

Units of X	MU_X /6	Units of Y	MU_Y /4
1	56 7	1	32 8
2	48 6	2	28 7
3	32 4	3	24 6
4	24 3	4	20 5
5	20 2.5	5	12 3
6	16 2	6	10 2.5
7	12 1.5	7	8 2

19. Refer to the preceding data. If the consumer has a money income of $52 and the prices of X and Y are $8 and $4 respectively, the consumer will maximize her utility by purchasing

    (A) 2 units of X and 7 units of Y

    (B) 5 units of X and 5 units of Y

    (C) 4 units of X and 5 units of Y

    (D) 3 units of X and 6 units of Y

    (E) 6 units of X and 3 units of Y

20. Suppose that MU_X/P_X is greater than MU_Y/P_Y. To maximize utility, consumers who are spending their entire budget should alter their consumption so that they purchase

    (A) less of X, but only if its price rises

    (B) more of Y, but only if its price rises

    (C) more of Y and less of X

    (D) neither; it should utilize the savings utility

    (E) more of X and less of Y

21. "Total cost," for an economist, includes

    (A) explicit and implicit costs, including a normal profit

    (B) neither implicit nor explicit costs

(C) implicit, but not explicit, costs

(D) explicit, but not implicit, costs

(E) explicit and implicit costs, including an economic profit

22. The main characteristic of supply in the short run is that

(A) barriers to entry prevent new firms from entering the industry

(B) the firm does not have sufficient time to change the size of its plant

(C) the firm does not have sufficient time to cut its rate of output to zero

(D) a firm does not have sufficient time to change the amounts of any of the resources it employs

(E) revenue is fixed

23. Marginal product is

(A) the increase in total output attributable to the employment of one more worker

(B) the increase in total revenue attributable to the employment of one more worker

(C) the increase in total product divided by the change in revenue

(D) the increase in total cost attributable to the employment of one more worker

(E) total product divided by the number of workers employed

24. The law of diminishing returns indicates that

(A) as revenue increases with each sale, total revenue declines

(B) as extra units of a variable resource are added to a fixed resource, marginal product will decline beyond some point

(C) because of economies and diseconomies of scale, a competitive firm's long-run average total cost curve will be U-shaped

(D) the demand for goods produced by purely competitive industries is downsloping

(E) beyond some point, the extra utility derived from additional units of a product will yield the consumer smaller and smaller extra amounts of satisfaction

Answer **Question 25** on the basis of the following output data for a firm. Assume that the amounts of all nonlabor resources are fixed.

Number of Workers	Units of Output
0	0
1	40
2	90
3	126
4	150
5	165
6	180

25. Refer to the preceding data. The marginal product of the sixth worker is

    (A) 180 units of output

    (B) 30 units of output

    (C) 45 units of output

    (D) 15 units of output

    (E) negative 15 units of output

26. Marginal product

    (A) diminishes at all levels of production

    (B) increases at all levels of production

    (C) may initially increase, then diminish, but never become negative

    (D) may initially increase, then diminish, and ultimately become negative

    (E) is always less than average product

27. If you owned a small farm, which of the following would be a fixed cost?

    (A) Farm workers

    (B) Flood insurance

    (C) Gasoline

(D) Pesticide

(E) Seed

28. If you operated a small pizzeria, which of the following would be a variable cost in the short run?

(A) Baking ovens

(B) Interest on business loans

(C) Annual lease payment for use of the building

(D) Cheese toppings

(E) Fire insurance

29. Marginal cost is the

(A) rate of change in total fixed cost that results from producing one more unit of output

(B) change in total cost that results from producing one more unit of output

(C) increase in revenue caused by one more unit being consumed

(D) change in average variable cost that results from producing one more unit of output

(E) change in average total cost that results from producing one more unit of output

30. Average fixed cost

(A) equals marginal cost when average total cost is at its minimum

(B) may be found for any output by adding average variable cost and average total cost

(C) at some point begins to increase as output reduces

(D) is graphed as a U-shaped curve

(E) declines continually as output increases

Individual Firm—Purely Competitive Market

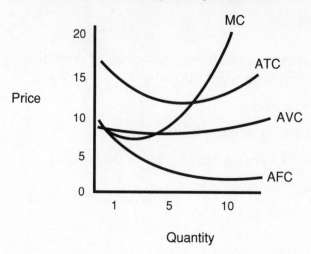

31. Refer to the preceding diagram. The vertical distance between ATC and AVC reflects

    (A) the law of diminishing returns

    (B) the break-even point

    (C) the average fixed cost at each level of output

    (D) marginal cost at each level of output

    (E) the presence of economies of scale

32. If a technological advance reduces the amount of labor needed to produce an increased level of output, then

    (A) the AVC curve will shift upward

    (B) the MC curve will shift upward

    (C) the ATC curve will shift downward

    (D) the AFC curve will shift upward

    (E) the cost curves will all be unaffected by the technological advance

Answer **Question 33** on the basis of the following cost data.

Output	Average Fixed Cost	Average Variable Cost
1	$50.00	$100.00
2	25.00	80.00
3	16.67	66.67
4	12.50	65.00
5	10.00	68.00
6	8.33	73.33
7	7.14	80.00
8	6.25	87.50

33. Based upon the preceding table, if the firm decided to increase its output from 6 to 7 units, by how much would its total costs rise?

(A) $170.00

(B) $80.00

(C) $6.67

(D) $120.02

(E) $108.02

34. In the short run, a purely competitive firm that seeks to maximize profit will produce

(A) where marginal revenue intersects demand

(B) where the demand and ATC curves intersect

(C) where total revenue exceeds total cost by the maximum amount

(D) that output where economic profits are zero

(E) at any point where the total revenue and total cost curves intersect

35. A firm reaches a breakeven point (normal profit position) where

    (A) marginal revenue cuts the horizontal axis

    (B) marginal cost intersects the average variable cost curve

    (C) total revenue equals total variable cost

    (D) total revenue and total cost are equal

    (E) total revenue equals all explicit costs

36. The MR = MC rule applies

    (A) to firms in all types of industries

    (B) to firms only in a natural monopoly

    (C) only when the firm is a "price taker"

    (D) only to monopolies

    (E) only to purely competitive firms

Answer **Question 37** on the basis of the following data confronting a firm.

Output	Marginal Revenue	Marginal Cost
0	—	—
1	$16	$10
2	16	9
3	16	13
4	16	17
5	16	21

37. Refer to the preceding data. If the firm's minimum average variable cost is $10, the firm's profit-maximizing level of output would be

    (A) 2

    (B) 3

    (C) 4

    (D) 5

    (E) 1

Firm's Costs

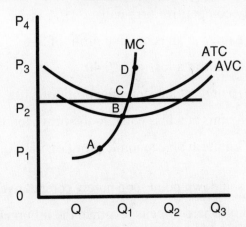

38. Refer to the preceding diagram for a purely competitive producer. The lowest price at which the firm should produce (as opposed to shutting down)

(A) is P_1

(B) is P_2

(C) is P_3

(D) is P_4

(E) is P_5

Answer **Question 39** on the basis of the following cost data for a firm that is selling in a purely competitive market.

Average Total Product	Average Fixed Cost	Average Variable Cost	Total Cost	Marginal Cost
1	$100.00	$17.00	$117.00	$17
2	50.00	16.00	66.00	15
3	33.33	15.00	48.33	13
4	25.00	14.25	39.25	12
5	20.00	14.00	34.00	13
6	16.67	14.00	30.67	14
7	14.29	15.71	30.00	26
8	12.50	17.50	30.00	30
9	11.11	19.44	30.55	35
10	10.00	21.60	31.60	41
11	9.09	24.00	33.09	48
12	8.33	26.67	35.00	56

39. Refer to the preceding data. If the market price for the firm's product is $42, the purely competitive firm will

(A) produce 8 units at an economic profit of $16

(B) produce 5 units at a loss of $10.40

(C) produce 10 units at an economic profit of $104

(D) produce 8 units at a loss equal to the firm's total fixed cost

(E) produce 7 units at an economic profit of $41.50

40. The short-run shutdown point for a purely competitive firm occurs

(A) at any point where price is less than the minimum AVC

(B) between the two breakeven points

(C) at any point where total revenue is greater than total cost

(D) at any point below normal profit

(E) at any point where the firm is not making an economic profit

Answer **Question 41** on the basis of the following cost data for a purely competitive seller.

Total Product Cost	Total Fixed Cost	Total Variable Cost	Total
0	$50	$0	$50
1	50	70	120
2	50	120	170
3	50	150	200
4	50	220	270
5	50	300	350
6	50	390	440

41. Refer to the preceding data. What is the marginal cost of the fifth unit of output?

    (A) $80

    (B) $90

    (C) $50

    (D) $70

    (E) $20

42. We would expect an industry to expand if firms in that industry are

    (A) meeting explicit and implicit costs

    (B) earning normal profits

    (C) earning economic profits

    (D) realizing an equality of total revenue and total costs

    (E) earning accounting profits

43. A firm is producing at an output where the revenue gain from the last unit produced is less than the cost of producing that additional unit. This firm is

    (A) producing more output than allocative efficiency requires

    (B) producing at an output that does not cover explicit costs

    (C) producing less output than allocative efficiency requires

    (D) realizing productive efficiency

    (E) producing an inefficient output, but we cannot say whether output should be increased or decreased

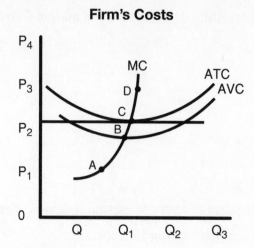

Firm's Costs

44. Refer to the preceding diagram. By producing at output level Q_1 in a purely competitive environment

    (A) the firm is operating below shut-down level

    (B) neither productive nor allocative efficiency is achieved

    (C) both productive and allocative efficiency are achieved

    (D) allocative efficiency is achieved, but productive efficiency is not

    (E) productive efficiency is achieved, but allocative efficiency is not

45. Refer to the preceding diagram. At output level Q_2 in a purely competitive environment

    (A) the firm is operating below shut-down level

    (B) resources are overallocated to this product and productive efficiency is not realized

    (C) resources are underallocated to this product and productive efficiency is not realized

    (D) productive efficiency is achieved, but resources are underallocated to this product

    (E) productive efficiency is achieved, but resources are overallocated to this product

46. "Public goods" refers to

    (A) any goods or services that society wants produced

    (B) goods whose production presumes large monopolistic corporations rather than small competitive firms

    (C) goods that cannot exclude consumers by price and are produced through the market system

    (D) goods produced at an efficient level of output due to elimination of competition

    (E) goods that are produced using minimal amounts of society's scarce resources

Market Model

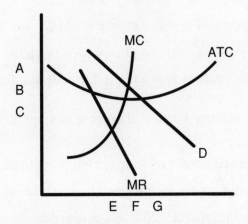

47. Refer to the preceding diagram. To maximize profits or minimize losses, this firm should produce

    (A) E units and charge price C

    (B) E units and charge price A

    (C) F units and charge price B

    (D) G units and charge price C

    (E) E units and charge price B

48. An important economic problem associated with pure monopoly is that, at profit-maximizing outputs, resources are

    (A) overallocated, because price exceeds marginal cost

    (B) overallocated, because price is less than demand

    (C) overallocated, because marginal cost exceeds price

    (D) underallocated, because price exceeds marginal cost

    (E) underallocated, because marginal cost exceeds price

49. When a monopolistically competitive firm is in long-run equilibrium

    (A) production takes place where ATC is minimized

    (B) marginal revenue equals marginal cost and price equals average total cost

    (C) economic profit is above minimum ATC

    (D) normal profit is zero and price equals marginal cost

    (E) economic profit is zero and price equals marginal cost

50. In the long run, new firms will enter a monopolistically competitive industry

    (A) provided economies of scale are being realized

    (B) even though losses are incurred in the short run

    (C) until minimum average total cost is achieved

    (D) as long as minimum AVC is met and shut-down is avoided

    (E) until economic profits are zero

51. Cartels are difficult to maintain in the long run because

    (A) they are illegal in all industrialized countries

    (B) firms realize that profits would increase if they secretly increase output

    (C) not all members are able to attain profitable output levels

    (D) it is more profitable for the industry to charge a lower price and produce more output

    (E) entry barriers are insignificant in oligopolistic industries

52. In the United States, professional football players earn much higher incomes than professional hockey players. This is because

    (A) most football players would be good hockey players while the reverse is not true

    (B) consumers have a greater demand for football games than for hockey games

    (C) there is a high degree of substitution of football for hockey games for most consumers

    (D) the total productivity of hockey players exceeds that of football players

    (E) most hockey players are foreign-born

53. Assume the Tutta Bulla restaurant is hiring labor in an amount such that the MRC of the last worker is $18 and the MRP is $22. On the basis of this information, we can say that

    (A) profits will be increased by hiring additional workers

    (B) profits will be increased by hiring fewer workers

    (C) marginal revenue product must exceed average revenue product

    (D) Tutta Bulla is maximizing profits

    (E) Tutta Bulla is operating below minimum AVC

Answer **Question 54** on the basis of the following marginal product data for resources A and B. The output of these resources sells in a purely competitive market at $1 per unit.

Inputs of A	MP_A	Inputs of B	MP_B
1	25	1	40
2	20	2	36
3	15	3	32
4	10	4	24
5	5	5	20
6	2	6	16
7	1	7	8

54. Refer to the preceding data. Assuming that the prices of resources A and B are $5 and $8 respectively, what is the profit-maximizing combination of resources?

    (A) 7 of A and 7 of B

    (B) 6 of A and 4 of B

    (C) 5 of A and 7 of B

    (D) 4 of A and 4 of B

    (E) 3 of A and 5 of B

Answer **Question 55** on the basis of the following data.

Quantity of Labor	MP of Labor	MRP of Labor	Quantity of Capital	MP of Capital	MRP of Capital
1	15	$45	1	8	$24
2	12	36	2	6	18
3	9	27	3	5	15
4	6	18	4	4	12
5	3	9	5	3	9
6	1	3	6	2	6

55. Refer to the preceding data. This firm is selling its product in

    (A) an imperfectly competitive market at prices that decline as sales increase

    (B) a purely competitive market at $3 per unit

    (C) a purely competitive market at $2 per unit

    (D) a pure monopoly at $4 per unit

    (E) an imperfectly competitive market at $3 per unit

Pollution Levels

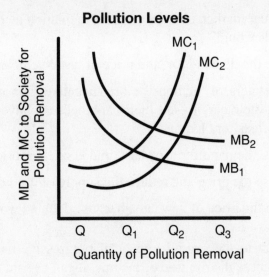

Quantity of Pollution Removal

56. Refer to the preceding diagram. Which of the following might shift the marginal benefit curve from MB_1 to MB_2?

   (A) A new government tax on pollution

   (B) Major new studies strongly linking cancer to pollution

   (C) Improved technology for reducing pollution

   (D) A change in consumer tastes for manufacturing goods

   (E) A decrease in the price of recycled goods

57. There is little incentive for a firm in a competitive environment to internalize spillover costs, as this would

   (A) cause it to forgo the diseconomies of agglomeration

   (B) shift its cost curves downward

   (C) put it at a competitive disadvantage compared to rival producers

   (D) make it subject to emission or effluent fees

   (E) shift its supply curve rightward

58. In the used car market, new government regulation increasing car quality standards would

    (A) reduce the demand for, and price of, used vehicles

    (B) give owners of "lemons" more incentive than owners of high-quality new cars to sell their cars, because buyers refuse to pay high prices for "lemons"

    (C) increase demand for used cars, and keep their prices low

    (D) increase the price and reduce the supply of used cars

    (E) reduce the price of new cars, because demand would decrease

59. With respect to the overall impact of progressive taxes and transfer payments on the distribution of income, it can be said that

    (A) taxes decrease, but transfers increase, income inequality

    (B) taxes increase, but transfers reduce, income inequality

    (C) both taxes and transfers decrease income inequality

    (D) both taxes and transfers increase income inequality

    (E) they cancel each other out, causing no change in the distribution of income

60. Differences in education and training

    (A) combine with differences in mental, physical, and inherited assets to produce income inequality

    (B) contribute little to income inequality in the United States

    (C) explain nearly all the income inequality in the United States

    (D) explain most, but not all, of the declining income inequality in the United States

    (E) were ignored as a key element of U.S. quota and affirmative action programs

Answer **Questions 61–63** based on the following information and graph.

The original supply and demand curves for this good are S1 and D. The government imposes an excise tax on the good such that P3 – Tax = P1. This tax shifts the supply curve from S1 to S2.

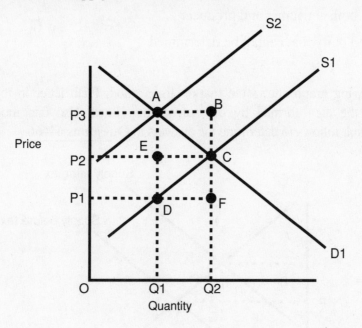

61. The area that represents the amount of tax collected by the government is equal to

    (A) ACD

    (B) EABC

    (C) P3BCP2

    (D) ABFD

    (E) P3ADP1

62. The efficiency (deadweight) loss in this market is equal to area

    (A) ACD

    (B) P3ADP1

    (C) EACB

    (D) ABFD

    (E) P3BCP2

63. In this scenario the tax burden would be borne by

(A) the consumer

(B) the producer

(C) the government

(D) both consumer and producer

(E) a party that cannot be determined

The following graph shows the market for a good. Each letter in the graph refers to the area formed by the surrounding lines. Use this model and the chart that follows to determine the answers to **Questions 64–66**.

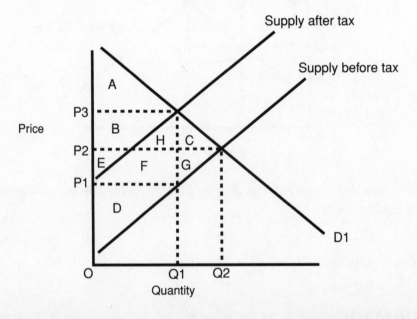

Answer	Consumer Surplus	Producer Surplus	Deadweight Loss
A	A	D	C + G
B	A + B	D + F	C + G
C	A + B + H + C	D + E + F + G	No loss
D	D + E + F + G	A + B + H + C	C + G
E	A + B	E + F + G	E

64. From the chart select the combination that represents consumer surplus, producer surplus, and deadweight loss before the tax is imposed.

    (A) A   (D) D
    (B) B   (E) E
    (C) C

65. From the chart select the combination that represents consumer surplus, producer surplus, and deadweight loss after the tax is imposed.

    (A) A   (D) D
    (B) B   (E) E
    (C) C

66. If production of the good creates air pollution, which combination from the chart would account for the real cost of the good?

    (A) A   (D) D
    (B) B   (E) E
    (C) C

The following game cube is for a duopoly and the payoffs associated with the decisions of two oligopolies, Firm X and Firm Y. Use the illustration to answer **Questions 67 and 68**.

FIRM X

	Strategy 1	Strategy 2
	$600 Million Profit	$400 Million Profit
FIRM Y Strategy 1	$300 Million Profit	$200 Million Profit
	$300 Million Profit	$0 Million Profit
Strategy 2	$50 Million Profit	$250 Million Profit

67. If Firm Y pursues strategy 2, what is the likely reaction of Firm X?

    (A) Firm X pursues the low price strategy and starts a price war.

    (B) Firm X has no correct strategy it can pursue.

(C) Firm X pursues strategy 2 as well.

(D) Firm X does not react, because strategy 1 continues to be in its best interest.

(E) Firm X pursues a strategy of overt collusion.

68. The decisions of Firm X based on the game cube can best be described as a behavior strategy known as

(A) "tit for tat"

(B) covert collusion

(C) strategic equilibrium

(D) a dominant strategy

(E) the dilemma

The following game cube is for a duopoly and the payoffs associated with the decisions of two oligopolies, Firm X and Firm Y. Use the illustration to answer **Questions 69 and 70**.

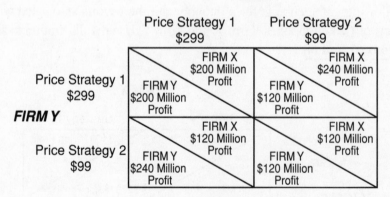

69. If Firm X chooses to touch off a price war, what is the likely outcome?

(A) Firm Y does not react but maintains its current pricing strategy 1.

(B) Firm X sees its profits rise to $240 million, increasing its market share.

(C) Firm Y matches the lower price, and both firms see their profits decline.

(D) Firm Y raises its prices above the $299 strategy to increase its profit margin and make up for the loss of market share.

(E) The reaction of Firm Y is not predictable given these profit outcomes.

70. The strategy behavior that this cube dictates is known as

(A) noncollusion

(B) "tit for tat"

(C) noncooperative collusion

(D) a dominant strategy

(E) oligopoly dilemma

71. The market equilibrium price of gasoline is $2.50 per gallon. If the government imposes a price cap of $2.00 per gallon, which of the following is likely to occur?

I.   The quantity supplied increases.

II. The quantity demanded increases.

III. The quantity supplied decreases.

IV. The quantity demanded decreases.

(A) I only   (D) II and III

(B) I and IV   (E) III only

(C) II only

72. The market equilibrium price of gasoline is $2.50 per gallon. If the government imposes a price floor of $3.00 per gallon, which of the following is likely to occur?

    I.   The quantity supplied increases.

    II.   The quantity demanded increases.

    III. The quantity supplied decreases.

    IV. The quantity demanded decreases.

    (A) I only   (D) III and IV

    (B) I and IV   (E) III only

    (C) II only

73. A government subsidy to the dairy industry is most likely to result in

    (A) a shortage of milk if the resulting price is above equilibrium

    (B) a shortage of product if the resulting price is at equilibrium

    (C) a surplus of milk if the resulting price is above equilibrium

    (D) a surplus of product if the resulting price is at equilibrium

    (E) an increase in the consumption of dairy products, and the consumer would enjoy the spillover benefits of milk drinking encouraged by the government

74. A government imposes a minimum wage law that is effectively at equilibrium. If the supply of labor increases, what is likely to occur in the new labor market?

    (A) Unemployment decreases.

    (B) Unemployment increases.

    (C) Labor wages decrease.

    (D) Labor wages increase.

    (E) The quantity of labor demanded increases.

75. If a firm has been disposing of its waste by burning it at no charge and Congress passes a new law banning the burning of garbage, what is the impact on price and output?

Price	Output
(A) Lower	Higher
(B) Lower	Lower
(C) Higher	Lower
(D) Higher	Higher
(E) No change	No change

76. The following headline appears in the newspaper: "OPEC meeting ends with several nations dropping membership." How might the price and output of oil be affected by the reported action of these OPEC nations?

Price	Output
(A) Lower	Higher
(B) Lower	Lower
(C) Higher	Lower
(D) Higher	Higher
(E) No change	No change

77. What is the U.S. government's role in the free market?

   I.   It regulates the food and drug industries.

   II. It provides a safety net for low- and no-income Americans.

   III. It owns and operates several media outlets.

   (A) I only

   (B) II only

   (C) I and II

   (D) I and III

   (E) II and III

78. Allan is known as a sharply dressed man who buys all his clothing at an exclusive men's shop. Allan's ability to purchase fine men's clothing would

    (A) remain the same if he lost his job, because Allan would have to keep up his image

    (B) decrease if he got a raise

    (C) remain unchanged, regardless of his income

    (D) change if he lost his job, forcing him to buy name brands

    (E) increase if he got a raise

79. Suppose two countries are each capable of producing two products. However, each specializes by producing the good for which it has a comparative advantage and then trades with the other country. Which of the following is most likely to result?

    (A) Both countries benefit from increased production of goods.

    (B) Unemployment increases in one country and decreases in the other.

    (C) Production is more efficient in one country but less efficient in the other.

    (D) The two countries become more independent of each other.

    (E) Both countries are harmed because productive inefficiency increases.

80. Which of the following is one reason government intervention to correct a market distortion might fail?

    (A) The government can supply only merit goods.

    (B) There is incomplete information regarding all the costs of intervention.

    (C) The laws of supply and demand are not relevant to government.

    (D) The opportunity cost of government intervention is zero.

    (E) The cost of service delivery is lower because of government efficiency.

CLEP MICROECONOMICS
PRACTICE TEST 1

ANSWER KEY

1. (C)	28. (D)	55. (B)
2. (C)	29. (B)	56. (B)
3. (A)	30. (E)	57. (C)
4. (C)	31. (C)	58. (D)
5. (C)	32. (C)	59. (C)
6. (C)	33. (D)	60. (A)
7. (D)	34. (C)	61. (E)
8. (C)	35. (D)	62. (A)
9. (B)	36. (A)	63. (D)
10. (E)	37. (B)	64. (C)
11. (B)	38. (B)	65. (A)
12. (B)	39. (C)	66. (C)
13. (E)	40. (A)	67. (D)
14. (E)	41. (A)	68. (D)
15. (E)	42. (C)	69. (C)
16. (C)	43. (A)	70. (B)
17. (A)	44. (C)	71. (D)
18. (B)	45. (B)	72. (B)
19. (C)	46. (C)	73. (E)
20. (E)	47. (B)	74. (B)
21. (A)	48. (D)	75. (C)
22. (B)	49. (B)	76. (A)
23. (A)	50. (E)	77. (C)
24. (B)	51. (B)	78. (D)
25. (D)	52. (B)	79. (A)
26. (D)	53. (A)	80. (D)
27. (B)	54. (C)	

DETAILED EXPLANATIONS OF ANSWERS

PRACTICE TEST 1

1. **(C)** Microeconomics is primarily focused on the components that make up the economy. In a free-market system, consumers, producers, government, and trade are the four main components.

2. **(C)** Economic efficiency is related to the average total cost of producing a good or providing a service. By extracting the maximum production from inputs, we realize minimum average total cost. This productive efficiency, when combined with allocative efficiency, contributes to the realization of the highest standard of living attainable for a society.

3. **(A)** The PPF curve is a model that demonstrates the economic reality that all inputs are not equal. It further demonstrates that we have choices in how our resources are employed in the production of alternative goods. In fact, as we exhaust our inputs they diminish in their productive capability, reducing at some point our total productivity, thereby raising our costs.

4. **(C)** As discussed in question 3, opportunity cost is the realization that scarcity causes us to make economic choices in how our limited resources are employed in production of alternative goods. As we choose to make one good, we sacrifice the value of the alternative choice.

5. **(C)** Box C represents the producer of goods and services that are brought (4) to product market D, and offered for sale to household A.

6. **(C)** Critical to the effectiveness of markets is that sellers of similar g/s are in competition for consumer expenditures. "Substitution" is the word employed by economists to describe the market reality that consumers are willing to replace a good or service whose price has increased with a like g/s.

7. **(D)** This is predicated upon the cross-elasticity formula. This formula states that as the price of a g/s decreases and the consumption of another g/s increases a degree of complement exists. Some students are tempted to conclude that C is a correct answer, but income change is not present and is necessary to conclude whether a g/s is inferior or normal/superior.

8. **(C)** A basic principle of demand is that price change causes a change in quantity demanded. Price up, Q_d down. Price down, Q_d up. The determinants of demand cause a shift in the demand curve. Be wary of this simple but effective trap!

9. **(B)** An increase in the costs of production inputs is a determinant of supply that causes the supply curve to move up and inward, representing higher overall prices. As prices rise, consumers will seek a substitute g/s. Since wine can be substituted for beer and its price has remained constant, consumers will shift some of their expenditure to wine.

10. **(E)** The equilibrium (market) price is the intersection point of the supply and demand curves. Trace the equilibrium point to the y-axis and a price of $2.50 is revealed. Trace the equilibrium point to the x-axis and a quantity of 250 gallons is revealed.

11. **(B)** A fundamental principle established by Adam Smith was the power of specialization, not only of individuals but nations as well. Specialization results in maximum output from resources, and contributes to economic efficiency, thus minimizing cost.

12. **(B)** This answer is based upon the least cost combination of labor and capital. We do not know the marginal product of labor and capital. All we do know is the various combinations of labor and capital that together yield 30 units of output, and the cost of each unit resource. So, by establishing the cost of the four various techniques, we can determine which is the least costly and when subtracted from our total revenue, $(30 \times 0.50 =)$ $15, yields the highest profit. The outcome of the four techniques can be viewed below.

Technique I, 4 labor ($8) + 2 capital ($6) = $14 and a profit of $1.

Technique II, 3 labor ($6) + 3 capital ($9) = $15 and $0 profit.

Technique III, 2 labor ($4) + 5 capital ($15) = $19 and a $4 loss.

Technique IV, 5 labor ($10) + 1 capital ($3) = $13 and
$2 economic profit.

13. **(E)** This answer combines cross-elasticity of income, consumer behavior and its impact on market forces, and the reaction of firms to profit. If consumer income increases, the demand for normal goods would increase. The resultant shift in demand would cause an increase in equilibrium price and quantity. The higher price and quantity would attract firms to the opportunity to obtain profit.

14. **(E)** Public goods (like a park or defense) are defined as g/s that are not divisible and are subject to free riders. Since division of the g/s is difficult, if not impossible, the incentive of profit is not present. Therefore, even though the demand for the g/s is clearly present, it would not be produced in a free market, as profit is not present and allocative efficiency cannot be determined.

15. **(E)** The simple price elasticity test determines the percentage of change in quantity demanded (0.20) divided by the percentage of change in price (0.10). If the quotient (2) is greater than 1, the demand is considered elastic. If the quotient is less than 1, it is classified as inelastic. This measurement tells firms how price-sensitive consumers are. The total revenue test would work as well; if total revenue goes up, the demand is elastic, and if the total revenue decreases, the demand is inelastic.

16. **(C)** This answer is based upon the cross-elasticity of demand formula. If the price of X goes up (+) and the demand for Y goes down (−), a negative quotient results, indicating a complementary relationship. If a positive quotient results, the g/s are substitutes, and if there is no change, the g/s are not related.

17. **(A)** The formula for cross-elasticity of income determines the percentage of change in quantity of good X divided by the percentage of change in the income of the consumer. If the quotient is positive, then the goods are considered normal/superior as the consumer chooses to buy more (as he or she can afford more). If income rises and the consumer buys less, the good is deemed inferior, as the consumer shifts his or her consumption to a superior comparative good.

18. **(B)** Marginal utility measures the change in total utility divided by the change in quantity. In this case, there is a change in total utility from 30 to 36, a change of 6. When divided by the quantity change of 1 (2 to 3 units = 1 unit), the marginal utility quotient is 6.

19. **(C)** This question requires the formula used to determine utility maximization of income, which determines the utility per dollar gained by the purchase of different goods when constrained by an income budget. This formula seeks to find a balance in satisfaction, as consumers do, when choosing the combination of goods to purchase within their limited income. The formula is $MU_x/P_x = MU_y/P_y$ = budget $. So, divide the MU at each quantity by the price of that good to obtain the MU per dollar of that good. When the MU per dollar of two or more goods is equal, and the combined quantity purchased is within the budget constraint, you have utility maximization. In this case, at 4 units of X you have a per dollar MU of 3 (24/$8 = 3), and at 5 units of Y you have an MU per dollar of 3 (12/$4 = 3), so the units per dollar are equal. The next step is to determine if this combination of goods is within the budget constraints. 4 units of X × $8 each = $32 spent, and 5 units of Y × $4 each = $20 spent, for a total of $52. MU per dollar of X = 3, MU per dollar of Y = 3 = $52 budget.

20. **(E)** This answer is predicated upon the utility-maximizing formula established in the previous question. As you increase the quantity purchased at a fixed price, the utility per dollar decreases. For example, if good X costs $2 per unit, and you increase your purchasing by one unit while MU decreases from 20 to 10, your per dollar MU would also decrease from 10 (20MU/$2) to 5 (10MU/$2).

21. **(A)** Economists determine costs and profits differently than accountants. An accountant views a firm's costs as consisting only of explicit (out of pocket) expenses, thus to them profit is total revenue (price × quantity) minus fixed and variable costs. The economist, however, includes implicit costs, like the lost value of alternative uses for startup capital, as well as entrepreneurial value (normal profit). So, breakeven point for an accountant would, to an economist, occur during economic loss, and when the economist observes breakeven point (includes normal profit) the accountant would see profit.

22. **(B)** This is a simple definition question. Short run is the length of time during which at least one input is fixed (plant size). Do not confuse this with increased or decreased utilization of existing plant size (24-hour, 7-day use) or shutdown of existing plants.

23. **(A)** This is another simple definition question. Marginal product formula is the change in total output divided by the change in input.

24. **(B)** This is a definition question. Even if we assume that all worker inputs are equal, at some point the relationship between the number of workers and the fixed plant (overcrowding) would result in inefficiencies that would cause the total product to decline. This realization is critical to understanding the shape of production cost curves.

25. **(D)** This answer is based upon the formula for determining marginal product. The change in total output divided by the change in input equals the marginal product. In this case, the change from 5 inputs to 6 inputs = 1 and total product increases from 165 to 180 = 15. 15 divided by 1 = a marginal product of 15.

26. **(D)** The formula from question 25, when applied to the relationship between increasing inputs and total productivity (opportunity costs increase, input quality diminishes as it is exhausted), yields the economic reality that at some point, the inputs of production will actually decrease total productivity, causing marginal productivity to become negative.

27. **(B)** By definition, insurance is a set premium that does not vary with a fixed farm size.

28. **(D)** Variable costs are defined as those costs that change as production increases or decreases. Fixed costs do not vary as output varies within a fixed plant structure. If the fixed plant changes in the long-run production process, fixed costs can increase or decrease, but then will become fixed at new levels.

29. **(B)** By definition, marginal cost is the change in the total cost divided by the change in quantity produced.

30. **(E)** By definition, AFC is the fixed cost divided by the total quantity produced. Mathematically, this number would constantly decline to infinity but the rate of decline would increasingly diminish.

31. **(C)** By definition, ATC = AFC + AVC. Therefore, ATC − AVC = AFC. This is the graphic model of this algebraic statement.

32. **(C)** Technical advance, by definition, means an improvement in the efficiency of output, i.e., you get more output from less input. Since costs are the inverse of productivity, as productivity increases, costs decrease.

Graphically, lower costs are represented by the curves moving downward towards the x-axis.

33. **(D)** By definition, fixed costs are constant, so the change in total variable cost between two different outputs would determine the change in total cost. Output × AVC = TVC. At 6 units, our total variable cost is 6 × $73.33 = $439.98. At 7 units of production, our total variable costs would be 7 × $80.00 = $560.00. The change in total cost caused by the increase in output from 6 to 7 units is $560.00 – 439.98 = $120.02.

34. **(C)** Profit equals total revenue minus total cost, and the given mission of this firm is to produce at the maximum profit in the short run.

35. **(D)** This answer requires knowledge of the basic definitions of breakeven and normal profit. Breakeven is the quantity and price combination wherein a firm's ATC = (average) price per unit sold. To an economist, normal profit would be included in ATC as an implicit cost of doing business, as noted earlier.

36. **(A)** Marginal revenue = marginal cost is a basic tenet of all firm behavior in any environment. The assumption is that all firms seek short run maximization of profit or minimization of loss. These profit/loss points always occur where MR = MC. If MR > MC, more profit (or less loss) could be had by increasing output. If MR < MC, more loss could be avoided (or profit might be obtained) by reducing output.

37. **(B)** This table verifies the MR = MC rule discussed previously. At output quantity 3, we come closest to MR = MC, and thus maximum profit. By adding MR at each level of output, we obtain total revenue of $48.00 with a total cost of $10 + 9 + 13 = $32.00, for a profit of $16.00. Any other output has less profit. At output quantity 4, output level TR is $64.00 and TC is $49.00, for a profit of $15.00—in other words, profits are not maximized as they are at MR = MC.

38. **(B)** At price 2, average price per product equals average variable cost. The firm is experiencing economic loss and its fixed and implicit costs are not being covered. However, its variable costs are being covered at this revenue level. A firm can continue to operate, in the short run, as long as inputs of production (like its workers) are being paid. It can keep the doors open in the hope that other firms will exit the market. If firms exit the market, prices would rise as industry supply decreased, and breakeven would

be attained. Remember, in a purely competitive market, P = D = MR and is perfectly elastic for the individual firm, which is a price taker. But the entire industry does have a downward sloping demand curve. So, as firms exit, the Industry Supply would shift left and price would rise in the industry, and to each individual firm.

39. **(C)** This question uses the MR = MC formula for profit maximization. If MR is $42, then this firm would produce at the 10 output level, where MC is $41 ($42 = $41). At 10 units, Total Revenue = $420.00 and Total Cost = 10 × (ATC) 31.60 = $316.00. TR – TC = profit, so $420.00 – $316.00 = $104.

40. **(A)** By definition, short-run shutdown point occurs where revenue does not cover the variable cost. If the workers are not paid, they will not work. If vendors are not paid, they don't deliver production resources. This soon results in the firm going out of business.

41. **(A)** By definition, marginal cost is the change in total cost/change in output. At output 4, TC is $270; at output 5, TC is $350. The change is $80/output change of 1 = MC = $80.

42. **(C)** Firms are attracted to economic profit, repelled by loss, and constant if at normal profit. So an industry would expand if existing firms were enjoying economic profit. Firms would enter until the industry returned to normal profit levels.

43. **(A)** A firm attains least cost maximum profit/minimum loss, where MR = MC. Since this firm is producing at an output where MR < MC, by reducing output, it would increase MR, decrease MC, and improve its profit/ loss position.

44. **(C)** In a purely competitive industry, productive efficiency (least costly) occurs where the price (which represents society's marginal benefit) quantity combination intersects minimum ATC, indicating lowest-cost production quantity. When quantity produced results in an intersection of price and marginal cost, allocative efficiency (quantity of goods most wanted by society) results. If price (MB) is greater than MC, underallocation of resources is occurring (increase production). If price (MB) is less than MC, then overallocation of resources is occurring (cut production).

45. **(B)** This firm is overproducing and overallocating resources, as Q_2 results in an ATC greater than revenue. Neither productive nor allocative efficiency is occurring; in fact, this firm has economic loss. Under these market conditions, the firm should reduce output to a Q_1 level and return to normal profit.

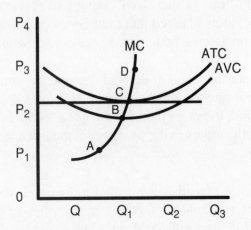

46. **(C)** By definition, public goods are indivisible and subject to free ridership, since price can't be used to determine use. Since profit cannot be obtained, there is no incentive to produce; at best, they would be underproduced.

47. **(B)** Firms maximize/minimize profits where MR = MC. MR = MC at quantity E and Price A. This firm will enjoy maximum economic profit at this price/demand and quantity.

48. **(D)** Pure monopolies produce a quantity that results in a price that underallocates resources, since the total revenue generated by doing this results in the highest profit margin.

49. **(B)** In long-run equilibrium, a monopolistically competitive firm can, at best, maintain normal profit, which occurs when MR = MC and price equals minimum ATC. If price rose above minimum ATC, economic profit would result, and firms would be attracted to the industry. If price fell below minimum ATC, economic loss would cause firms to exit the industry until equilibrium was attained.

50. **(E)** Due to ease of entrance and exit, as well as high levels of competition present in this market model, economic profit attracts firms, and economic loss repels firms until long-run equilibrium occurs, when price/ quantity equals minimum ATC.

51. **(B)**   Cartels are oligopolies acting in collusion that obtain monopoly status through their use of quotas to control quantity produced. High prices and economic profits are attained as a result. By secretly cheating on their cartel partners, they obtain the higher prices and increase their share of the economic profit. This is successful only in the short run, since in the long run prices would fall due to increased output and (assumed) constant demand. As cartel members realized that members were cheating, they would return to competition and the cartel would cease to function.

52. **(B)**   Wages are the result of derived demand. Assume that the supply of two goods (sports entertainment) is equal. If the demand for one sport is greater than the other, the price paid for the good would be higher. This reflects in the cost of the inputs to the producer in the labor market for football and hockey players.

53. **(A)**   Comparing Marginal Revenue Product and Marginal Resource Cost (MRP = MRC) is another method of determining maximum profit (similar to MR = MC concept), this time by balancing the marginal cost of resource inputs to the marginal revenue those resources generate for the firm. In the case of Tutta Bulla, the revenue generated at this level of output, while profitable, is not maximum profit. By producing more units, the marginal cost will rise, yet profits will also grow until MRP = MRC.

54. **(C)**   This question employs the formulas introduced in question 53. However, an additional formula has been added. In this case, it is necessary to balance the Marginal Productivity of two different inputs of production (labor and capital, for instance) with the marginal revenue they generate at various output levels. The formula is stated as MPA/price of A = MPB/price of B = marginal revenue product. Therefore, at units of A, 5 (MP)/$5 (5 units × $1 each) equals 7 units of B 8 (MP)/$8 (8 units × $1 each) = 1 = MRP of 1.

55. **(B)**   This is another method of testing your knowledge of the MRP formula, and combines it with knowledge of price structure of firms in different competitive market structures. Since MRP of labor = MP of labor × price of each unit produced, at 1 unit of labor MRP = 15 × $x = $45. Therefore, x = $3 price per unit. This quotient is the same at all output levels of labor. It is also true for the MP of capital and MRP of capital. 1 unit of capital has an MP of 8 units, so MRP = 8 × $x = $24; x = $3 price per unit. Since the price of each unit of production remains at $3, no matter the level of output, it must be a firm in a purely competitive market. Only in the

purely competitive market is price perfectly inelastic and equal to marginal revenue.

56. **(B)** Marginal Benefit reflects society's overall satisfaction with a g/s at various price quantity combinations—in this case, clean air and water. Marginal Cost is the cost of producing that clean air and water in those various combinations. So, as in all other free markets, equilibrium occurs when the cost of supplying clean air and water equals society's willingness to pay that price quantity combination. A change in MB is, in essence, an increase in demand for clean air and water. Only answer (B) would stimulate an increase in the demand for clean air and water. Since the demand would increase, quantity supplied would increase, and the price paid by society would rise.

57. **(C)** A spillover cost is a cost of production not borne directly by the producer or the consumer of a g/s. Society bears that cost, as in air pollution—if a firm in a competitive industry chose to bear the cost of pollution, its profits would diminish or it would have to raise its price. Since rival firms would not lose profits or have to raise their price (consumers would substitute the cheaper g/s), they would grow in strength.

58. **(D)** Again, this question concerns the impact that government intervention, in the form of taxation or regulation, has on a firm's cost structure, and thus market equilibrium. If government required sellers of used cars to guarantee higher reliability requirements, this would increase the cost of supplying cars to the consumer. These higher overall costs would shift the supply curve up and to the left. The resultant new market equilibrium would be at a higher price, with few cars demanded and supplied.

59. **(C)** Both progressive taxes and transfer payments, by definition, collect money from higher incomes and redistribute that money to lower incomes. Especially in the case of an increasing marginal income tax (the more one earns, the greater the percentage of tax) these are income-leveling activities.

60. **(A)** Derived demand significantly determines labor prices in a free-labor market. Differences in education and training make a worker more productive (MRP) and/or increasingly scarce (MRC). When a tight supply of highly skilled labor is combined with a high demand for that worker, a high price is paid. Since income is a great determinant of wealth, these factors in a free labor market would contribute to income inequality.

61. **(E)** Because of the higher price imposed upon the market by the excise tax, a lower quantity of the good is demanded and supplied. The area P3ADP1 represents the new equilibrium price times the new equilibrium quantity, and is equal to the amount of the tax burden.

62. **(A)** Area ACD represents the loss of efficiency attained by market equilibrium without government interference. This area represents the loss of quantity times the price no longer attained and indicates that the marginal utility is greater than the marginal cost.

63. **(D)** Because the price elasticities of supply and demand are equal, the tax burden is equally divided between the two participants in the market. If the demand curve was more price inelastic (steeper), the producer could shift an unequal burden of the tax to the consumer, because the consumer would not reduce consumption as significantly.

64. **(C)** This is a good illustration of a marketplace with no government interference. A free market results in the greatest possible total satisfaction (Consumer surplus + Producer surplus). This is why the competitive free market results in both allocative and productive efficiency, with no deadweight loss.

65. **(A)** Once the government levies a tax, the marketplace is distorted and inefficiency results (neither allocative nor productive efficiency). Area BHEF is the total burden of tax, area C + G is the efficiency loss, area A is the new consumer surplus, and area D is the new producer surplus.

66. **(C)** Accounting for a negative externality like air pollution is a major justification for government interference in the marketplace. The tax represents the cost of cleanup or the value of the lost clean air to society as a whole—a cost borne by parties not involved in the production of the good. Therefore, the new higher price more accurately reflects the cost of the good.

67. **(D)** Firm Y cannot win any price war because the price outcomes favor Firm X. A lower price damages Firm X because its revenues drop from $600 million to $300 million. However, the damage done to Firm Y is greater because its profits fall from $300 million to $50 million. Also, Firm X cannot alter its strategy because no other outcome results in the profits derived from inaction.

68. **(D)**   This scenario is known as a dominant strategy. Firm X is able to determine its greatest profit with no regard to the action of rival Firm Y, and Firm Y has no strategy that can improve its profit.

69. **(C)**   Firm Y has no choice but to match the lower price strategy; otherwise, it loses market share and watches its rival's profits grow. This is a classic price war scenario. It also helps to explain the kink in the oligopoly model and why firms will not necessarily follow a rival to a higher price (gain market share) but will follow a rival to a lower price (loss of market share).

70. **(B)**   The phrase "tit for tat" is another way to say that because of pricing outcomes, firms have a "you go low, we go low" mandate from the market. Neither firm enjoys an advantage with the customer or a cost structure that a lower price cannot overcome.

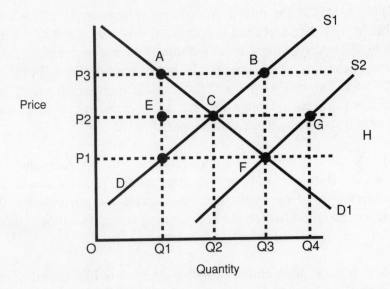

71. **(D)**   The result is a shortage. Use the preceding model to more easily see the effect of a price cap set below free market equilibrium. If the free market price is P2 ($2.50) and the price cap is P1 ($2.00), the quantity supplied moves from point C to point D, a decrease. At the same time the quantity demanded moves from point C to point F, an increase. When Qs is less than Qd, the result is a shortage in the amount of Q1 – D – F – Q3.

72. **(B)**   The result is a surplus. Use the model preceding explanation 71 to more easily see the effect of a price floor above equilibrium. If the market price is P2 ($2.50) and the price minimum is P3 ($3.00), the quantity

supplied moves from point C to point B, an increase. At the same time the quantity demanded moves from point C to point A, a decrease. When Qd is less than Qs, the result is a surplus in the amount of Q1 – A – B – Q3.

73. **(E)** A subsidy to dairy producers reduces their cost of production and shifts the supply from S1 to S2. The resulting lower price of dairy products increases the quantity demanded from C to F. The country enjoys the benefits of more dairy products in people's diets.

74. **(B)** Again, use the model preceding explanation 71 to see the answer. If the government sets the minimum wage at P2, market equilibrium C is attained. If the supply of labor shifts to S2, in a free market the increase in labor lowers wages to P1 and more workers are hired. However, because employers cannot pay below the minimum wage, they do not hire Q2 to Q3 additional workers, and higher unemployment occurs.

75. **(C)** Again, use the model preceding explanation 71 to see the answer. This firm's product generates a spillover cost that is not borne by the firm but by the society whose air is polluted. When a ban is placed on the firm, it must bear the cost of cleanup. The higher costs shift the supply curve from S2 to S1. The market price of the product increases from P1 to P2. At the higher price, the quantity demanded decreases from F to C, and the firm's output responds by decreasing from Q3 to Q2.

76. **(A)** A cartel attempts to empower itself with a monopoly's price-making ability. By using a quota to control output, a cartel attains an artificial undersupply of the marketplace and drives the price higher. When nations leave the OPEC cartel, thus eliminating its quota, oil producers increase their output and the price of oil decreases.

77. **(C)** The U.S. government provides safety nets like Social Security, unemployment, and temporary assistance to needy families. It also serves as a regulator through agencies like the Food and Drug Administration (FDA), the Federal Communications Commission (FCC), and the Federal Trade Commission (FTC). The government does not own and operate media companies (although it does subsidize them).

78. **(D)** This is largely an issue of cross-elasticity of income. With a reduced income Allan likely could afford name-brand goods; however, should his income continue to decline, he would be forced to switch to inferior goods.

79. **(A)** Comparative advantage demonstrates the efficiency that results from specialization. As individuals, as well as nations, specialize, their outputs increase relative to their inputs. Therefore, the combined output for the two countries increases. This increase in goods increases the standard of living in both nations.

80. **(D)** Remember, even though legislation may be well intentioned, it often suffers from issues such as recognition and operational lags. Also, diseconomies of scale occur, as well as "union" costs and good old "pork barrel" add-ons.

▼
PRACTICE
TEST 2

This test is also on CD-ROM in our special interactive TEST*ware*® for the CLEP Principles of Microeconomics exam. It is highly recommended that you first take this exam on computer. You will then have the additional study features and benefits of enforced time conditions, individual diagnostic analysis, and instant scoring.

CLEP Microeconomics

PRACTICE TEST 2

TIME: 90 Minutes
80 Questions

(Answer sheets appear in the back of this book.)

DIRECTIONS: Each of the questions or incomplete statements below is followed by five suggested answers or completions. Select the best answer for each question and then fill in the corresponding oval on the answer sheet.

---

1. The study of economics is primarily concerned with which of the following?

    (A) The allocation of scarce resources relative to unlimited wants

    (B) The equitable distribution of goods relative to income

    (C) The minimal provision of basic human needs

    (D) A balance between the cost of production and economic profits

    (E) Regulation of corporate profits and production pollution

Use the following graph to answer **Questions 2 and 3**.

Production Possibilities Frontier Curve

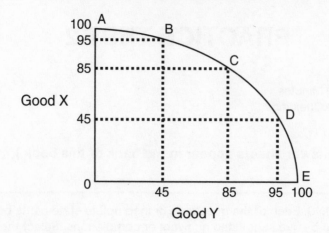

2. The opportunity cost of increasing the output of good Y from 85 to 95 units is how many units of good X?

    (A) 45

    (B) 1

    (C) 10

    (D) 40

    (E) Opportunity cost does not exist

3. A combination of 45 units of good Y and 45 units of good X is

    (A) productively efficient but allocatively inefficient

    (B) impossible to attain in the short run

    (C) possible in the long run with economic growth

    (D) the best combination because the trade-off ratio is 1 to 1

    (E) a possible combination of outputs but represents an inefficient use of resources

4. Based on the following graph of Firm X, select the most accurate statement.

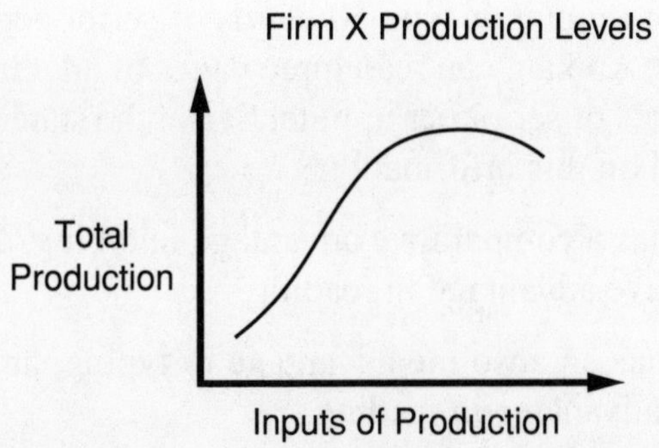

Firm X Production Levels

Total Production

Inputs of Production

(A) Firm X has a constant cost of production.

(B) Firm X's marginal cost increases at a constant rate.

(C) Firm X should increase its resource input units to its maximum.

(D) Firm X is better off producing at a low level.

(E) At some point, as Firm X adds more inputs, its total output decreases.

5. Based on the following graph, select the most accurate statement.

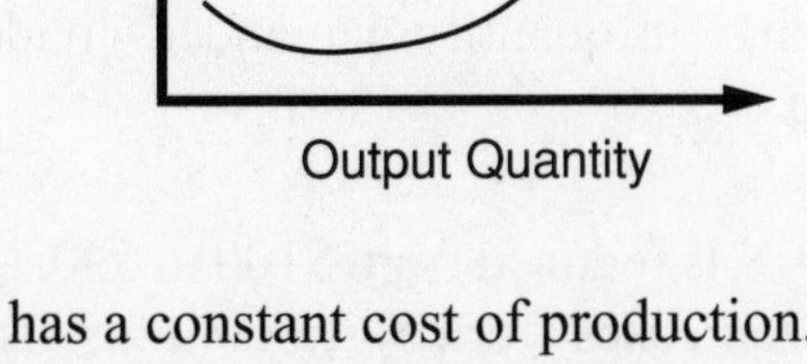

Firm X Marginal Cost Structure

Cost

Output Quantity

(A) Firm X has a constant cost of production.

(B) At some point Firm X's marginal cost increases at an increasing rate.

(C) Firm X should increase its output quantity to its maximum level.

(D) Firm X is better off producing at its lowest level.

(E) As Firm X increases its total output, its marginal costs never decrease.

6. A business owner hires two administrative assistants, assigning them the tasks of reading advertising proposals and typing commercial scripts on a computer. One of the aides, Obiwan, can read one page of advertising per minute or type 50 words of script per minute, and the other assistant, Anikan, can read three pages of advertising per minute or type 60 words of script per minute. Select the statement that is most accurate based on this information.

    (A) Obiwan has a comparative advantage in typing, and Anikan has a comparative advantage in reading.

    (B) Obiwan has an absolute advantage in typing, and Anikan has an absolute advantage in reading.

    (C) Obiwan has an absolute advantage in reading, and Anikan has a comparative advantage in typing.

    (D) Obiwan has a comparative advantage in both reading and typing.

    (E) Obiwan has an absolute advantage in both reading and typing.

7. The basic formula for the coefficient of the price elasticity of demand is

    (A) absolute decline in quantity demanded divided by absolute increase in price

    (B) percentage change in quantity supplied divided by percentage change in price

    (C) absolute decline in price divided by absolute increase in quantity demanded

    (D) percentage change in price divided by percentage change in quantity demanded

    (E) percentage change in quantity demanded divided by percentage change in price

8. The price of product X is reduced from $100 to $90, and as a result, the quantity demanded increases from 50 to 60 units. Therefore, demand for product X in this price range

    (A) has declined

    (B) is of unit elasticity

    (C) has an inelastic coefficient of 0.2

(D) has an elastic coefficient of 0.2

(E) has an elastic coefficient of 2

9. Assume that a firm has the following demand and total revenue curves for its product. The firm can draw what conclusion about the impact a price change will have on its total revenue?

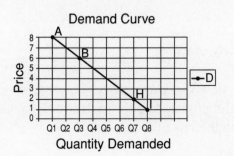
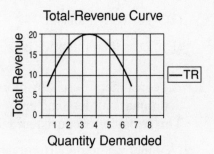

(A) Any increase in price will cause its total revenue to increase.

(B) Any decrease in price will cause its total revenue to increase.

(C) Any change in price will have a constant rate of effect on its total revenue.

(D) If the firm lowers its price from A ($8) to B ($7), its total revenue will decrease.

(E) If the firm lowers its price from A ($8) to B ($7), its total revenue will increase.

10. A company that produces an athletic drink sees its profits reduced because of a tax increase. If the company increases the price to its customers and as a result finds that its total revenue increases, then the price elasticity of demand for its product is classed as

(A) inelastic

(B) elastic

(C) unit elastic

(D) perfectly inelastic

(E) less than the price elasticity of its supply

11. Referring to the information in Question 10, if the same company increases its output and finds that its total revenue has decreased, it is operating in which portion of its demand curve?

(A) Inelastic

(B) Elastic

(C) Unit elastic

(D) Perfectly inelastic

(E) Less than the price elasticity of its supply

12. As consumers purchase more of a good or service, they enjoy each additional unit less and are willing to pay less for each additional unit. This behavior is consistent with the law of

(A) increasing opportunity cost

(B) diminishing returns

(C) total-revenue test

(D) diminishing marginal utility

(E) diminishing revenue product

13. The first Powerade drink yields Jeanette 18 units of utility, and the second drink yields her an additional 12 units of utility. Her total utility from three Powerade drinks is 39 units of utility. What is the marginal utility of the third drink?

(A) 26   (D) 38

(B) 6   (E) 13

(C) 9

14. The theory of consumer behavior assumes that

(A) total utility increases at an increasing rate

(B) consumers behave rationally, maximizing their satisfaction

(C) consumers have unlimited money incomes

(D) consumers do not know how much marginal utility they obtain from successive units of various products

(E) marginal utility increases at a constant rate

15. An economist predicts that a consumer will seek to maximize utility by allocating money income so that the

    (A) elasticity of demand on all products purchased is the same

    (B) marginal utility obtained from the last dollar spent on each product is the same

    (C) total utility derived from each product consumed is the same

    (D) marginal utility of the last unit of each product consumed is the same

    (E) inelastic goods are of greater importance than elastic goods

16. Suppose the marginal utility of product X divided by its price exceeds the marginal utility of product Y divided by its price. To maximize utility, consumers spending all their money income should buy which of the following?

    (A) Less of X only if its price rises

    (B) More of Y only if its price rises

    (C) More of Y and less of X

    (D) More of X and less of Y

    (E) Not enough information to determine

Use the following table to answer **Questions 17 and 18**.

The product schedules show the amounts of additional satisfaction (marginal utility) a consumer gets from successive quantities of products X and Y.

Product X		Product Y	
Units	Marginal Utility	Units	Marginal Utility
1	58	1	32
2	48	2	28
3	32	3	24
4	24	4	20
5	20	5	12
6	16	6	10
7	8	7	4

17. If the consumer has a money income of $52 and the prices of products X and Y are $8 and $4, respectively, the consumer maximizes utility by purchasing

(A) 2 units of X and 7 units of Y

(B) 5 units of X and 5 units of Y

(C) 4 units of X and 5 units of Y

(D) 6 units of X and 3 units of Y

(E) 7 units of X and 7 units of Y

18. If the consumer's income increases to $84 dollars and the products' prices remain the same, the consumer maximizes utility by purchasing

(A) 2 units of X and 7 units of Y

(B) 5 units of X and 5 units of Y

(C) 4 units of X and 5 units of Y

(D) 6 units of X and 3 units of Y

(E) 7 units of X and 7 units of Y

19. If a perfect competitor has a market price of $10, an average variable cost of $9, and an average total cost of $11, the best decision it can make is to

(A) continue to produce in the short run

(B) raise its price to at least $11

(C) shut down production immediately

(D) continue producing in the long run, even if its price and costs do not change

(E) produce fewer goods in the short run

20. Why does the perfect competitor described in question 19 behave as it does?

(A) It is not making a normal profit, so it should exit the industry in the short run.

(B) It is earning a normal rate of return because it is covering its average variable cost.

(C) If it reduces output, its average total cost will fall until it returns to normal profit.

(D) It remains in business in the belief that less efficient firms will exit the industry, prices will rise and normal profit will occur.

(E) By raising the price of the good to $11, it generates a small $1 profit per unit.

21. Diseconomies of scale are said to be present in an industry when

   (A) long-run average total cost remains constant as output increases

   (B) long-run average total cost increases as output increases

   (C) long-run average total cost decreases as output increases

   (D) input and output increase at the same rate

   (E) short-run average total cost remains constant as output increases

22. Economies of scale are said to be present in an industry when

   (A) long-run average total cost remains constant as output increases

   (B) long-run average total cost increases as output increases

   (C) long-run average total cost decreases as output increases

   (D) input and output increases at the same rate

   (E) short-run average total cost remains constant as output increases

23. Constant return to efficiencies of scale is said to be present in an industry when

   (A) long-run average total cost remains constant as output increases

   (B) long-run average total cost increases as output increases

   (C) long-run average total cost decreases as output increases

   (D) input and output increase at the same rate

   (E) short-run average total cost remains constant as output increases

24. The following long-run average total cost curve applies to which type of economy?

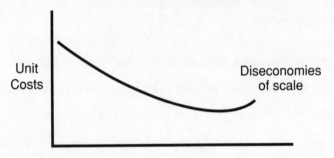

Economies of Scale,
Long-Run Average Total Cost

(A) Purely competitive firms

(B) Oligopoly

(C) Monopolistically competitive firms

(D) Both A and C

(E) Both B and C

25. The following long-run average total cost curve applies to which type of economy?

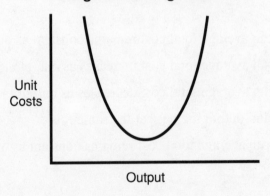

Economies of Scale,
Long-Run Average Total Cost

(A) Purely competitive firms

(B) Oligopoly

(C) Monopolistically competitive firms

(D) Both A and C

(E) Both B and C

26. Producer surplus is best illustrated by which of the following?

(A) As the equilibrium price of good X increases, the quantity supplied increases.

(B) When the government imposes a price cap below equilibrium, producer X refuses to remain in business.

(C) When the government imposes a price cap below equilibrium, producer X continues to bring his good to market.

(D) As the equilibrium price of good X decreases, the quantity supplied decreases.

(E) Producers feel safe adding a new tax to the consumer price.

27. Which of the following increases the demand for grapes?

(A) An increase in the price of apples, because they are a substitute

(B) An increase in the price of lettuce, because lettuce and grapes are complementary goods

(C) An increase in the cost of fertilizer to grape growers

(D) A decrease in incomes, because grapes are a normal good

(E) Medical research demonstrating that apples are better for your health than grapes

Use the following model to answer **Questions 28 and 29**.

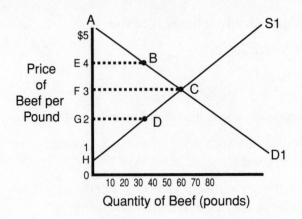

28. Which of the following is the area of consumer surplus?

    (A) ABE   (D) ACH

    (B) ACF   (E) FCH

    (C) ACDG

29. Which of the following is the area of producer surplus?

    (A) ABE   (D) ACH

    (B) ACF   (E) FCH

    (C) ACDG

30. Characteristics of a pure public good include which of the following?

    I.   Consumers cannot be excluded from consuming the good.

    II. Consumption of the good can be divided into individual portions.

    III. Price rationing is present in the market for the good.

    (A) I   (D) I and II

    (B) II   (E) II and III

    (C) III

31. If the variable cost for a firm's output decreases, which result is most likely?

    (A) The firm increases its output.

    (B) The marginal cost curve increases at all levels of output.

    (C) The firm exits the industry.

    (D) Average fixed costs decrease.

    (E) The market price of the good rises.

32. A monopoly is different from a purely competitive firm in that it

    (A) has a horizontal average total cost curve

    (B) is guaranteed a normal profit

    (C) has no average total cost curve

    (D) has a horizontal demand curve

    (E) has a marginal revenue curve that lies below its demand curve

33. In the long run, perfectly competitive firms

    (A) earn a normal profit

    (B) earn no profit

    (C) have no demand curve

    (D) may earn an economic profit

    (E) are guaranteed a greater-than-normal rate of return

34. If perfectly competitive firms are earning short-run economic profits, then

    (A) all firms increase their output

    (B) firms exit the industry

    (C) firms enter the industry

    (D) change does not occur

    (E) firms attain productive efficiency

Use the following model to answer **Questions 35–37**.

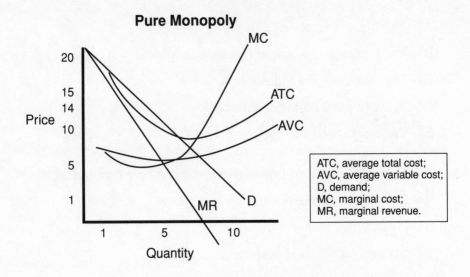

Pure Monopoly

ATC, average total cost;
AVC, average variable cost;
D, demand;
MC, marginal cost;
MR, marginal revenue.

35. What quantity does the firm produce?

   (A) Nothing, because it is in economic loss

   (B) 10 units

   (C) 5 units

   (D) 1 unit

   (E) 7 units, to attain allocative efficiency

36. Select the untrue statement regarding the pure monopoly.

   (A) It is possible to have long-run economic profit.

   (B) It will operate at an output quantity where MR = MC.

   (C) It will not operate at allocative efficiency.

   (D) It will not operate at productive efficiency.

   (E) It will set the price of the good.

37. If the firm chooses to price discriminate, then

    (A) it increases its quantity to 10 to sell all it can

    (B) it lowers its output from a productively efficient level of 7

    (C) its profits decrease because the demand is reduced by the now higher price

    (D) it raises the price to its last customer to $20

    (E) it sells all it can at a fixed price of $20

38. An industry produces at an output level greater than the socially optimum one when

    (A) the industry is a monopoly

    (B) negative externalities are present and unaccounted for

    (C) a tax equal to a negative externality is being charged

    (D) the good produced is a private one

    (E) positive externalities are present and unaccounted for

39. If a subsidy is eliminated from a public good that reduces its marginal social benefit, which of the following is likely to occur?

    (A) Production increases.

    (B) Social costs of the good decrease.

    (C) Optimal quality of the good decreases.

    (D) Optimal quantity of the good decreases.

    (E) The cost of production decreases.

Use the following model to answer **Questions 40–42**.

Monopsonist Labor Market

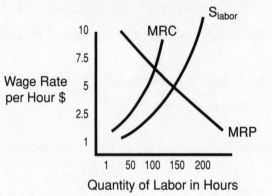

Quantity of Labor in Hours

40. In the labor market shown, the wage rate for a competitive market would be how many dollars per hour?

    (A) $7.50

    (B) $5.00

    (C) $2.50

    (D) Between $1.50 and $9.00

    (E) $8.00

41. In the labor market shown, the wage rate for a monopsonist would be how many dollars per hour?

    (A) $7.50

    (B) $5.00

    (C) $2.50

    (D) Between $1.50 and $9.00

    (E) $1.00

42. The monopsonist increases profits by

    (A) overproducing and overcharging, because it is a monopoly.

    (B) producing to a level where S = MRP.

    (C) producing to a level where MRP = MRC and paying $7.50 per hour.

    (D) producing where MRP = MRC and paying $2.50 per hour.

    (E) employing 150 workers and paying them $2.50 while the value of their product is $7.50.

43. The driving force behind mergers and acquisitions by firms (synergy) is to increase economic efficiency by

    (A) decreasing average total cost through an increase in economies of scale

    (B) increasing average total cost through an increase in economies of scale

    (C) decreasing output to reduce marginal cost and equalize price

    (D) increasing economic profits but decreasing consumer demand

    (E) increasing consumer surplus by decreasing price

Use the following model to answer **Questions 44 and 45**.

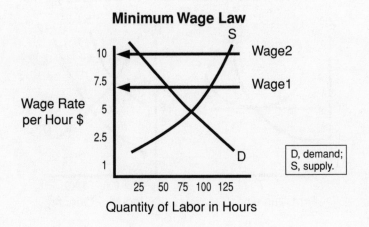

Minimum Wage Law

44. If Congress amends the minimum wage law to lower the rate per hour, what is the most likely effect on employment, based on the information provided?

    (A) Employment decreases.

    (B) Wages increase.

    (C) A shortage of labor occurs.

    (D) Employment and wages increase.

    (E) Employment increases.

45. If the minimum wage falls below equilibrium, what is the most likely effect on employment, based upon the information provided?

    (A) Employment decreases.

    (B) Wages increases.

    (C) A shortage of labor occurs.

    (D) Employment and wages increase.

    (E) Employment increases.

Use the following model to answer **Questions 46 and 47**.

Purely Competitive Firm and Industry

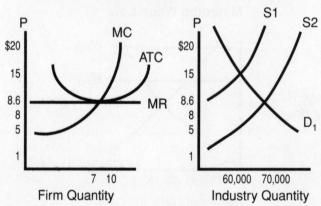

46. The relationship depicted in this purely competitive firm and industry indicate that

(A) Firms have exited the industry because prices were too low.

(B) The individual firm lowered its price and increased its market share.

(C) Firms have exited the industry, and productive efficiency has resulted.

(D) Firms have entered the industry, and the market price has fallen.

(E) Firms have entered the industry, and the individual firm's output has increased.

47. Before the industry change in supply, all the following were true EXCEPT

(A) productive efficiency was not present

(B) the firm was in economic profit

(C) allocative efficiency was not attained

(D) the firm was in normal profit

(E) firms had not had time to enter the market

48. If a consumer's income rises and the demand for good X falls, then

(A) good X has no complements

(B) the price has fallen for complements to good X

(C) good X is an inferior good

(D) good X is a normal good

(E) good X is price inelastic

49. Monopolistic competition is characterized by a(n)

(A) few dominant firms and low entry barriers

(B) large number of firms and substantial entry barriers

(C) ability to maintain long-run economic profit

(D) large number of firms and low entry barriers

(E) few dominant firms and substantial entry barriers

50. A monopolistically competitive industry combines elements of both competition and monopoly. The monopoly element stems from

   (A) the ability to earn long-run economic profit

   (B) the likelihood of collusion

   (C) high barriers to entry

   (D) product differentiation

   (E) mutual interdependence in decision making

Use the following model to answer **Questions 51–53**.

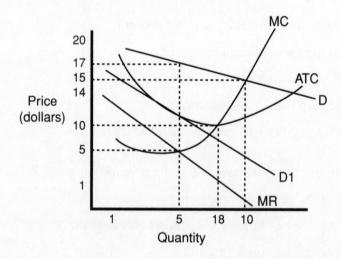

51. In the short run, the monopolistically competitive firm charges what price to maximize profits?

   (A) $17   (D) $5

   (B) $15   (E) $20

   (C) $9

52. In the short run, the monopolistically competitive firm produces at what output to maximize profits?

    (A) 1

    (B) 5

    (C) 7

    (D) 10

    (E) 17

53. In the long run, the monopolistically competitive firm produces at what price and output to maximize profits?

    (A) $1 and 10

    (B) $10 and 5

    (C) $14 and 10

    (D) $15 and 10

    (E) $20 and 1

54. If the U.S. government places an import tariff on foreign steel, which of the following is the most likely result?

    (A) Domestic steel workers lose their jobs.

    (B) Profits for domestic steel producers fall.

    (C) The supply of domestic steel falls.

    (D) Domestic steel prices fall.

    (E) Prices for products made of steel increase.

Use the following price strategy matrix to answer **Questions 55–57**.

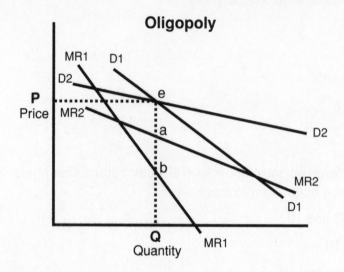

55. Assume a noncollusive firm is initially at equilibrium e with price P and quantity Q. Select the most true statement.

    (A) Demand curve D_1 assumes that rivals will match any price change initiated by this oligopolist.

    (B) Demand curves D_1 and D_2 both assume that rivals will ignore any price change initiated by this oligopolist.

    (C) Demand curves D_1 and D_2 both assume that rivals will match any price change initiated by this oligopolist.

    (D) Demand curve D_2 assumes that rivals will match any price change initiated by this oligopolist.

    (E) Demand curve D_1 assumes that rivals will not match any price change initiated by this oligopolist.

56. Assume a noncooperative firm is initially at equilibrium e with price P and quantity Q. If the firm's rivals ignore any price increase but match any price reduction, the firm's demand curve is

    (A) D_1eD_2

    (B) D_2eD_1

    (C) D_1eD_1

    (D) D_2eD_2

    (E) MR_2aMR_1

57. Assume that the firm is initially in equilibrium at point e where the equilibrium price and quantity are P and Q. If the firm's rivals ignore any price increase but match any price reduction, the firm's marginal revenue curve is

(A) D_1eD_2

(B) D_2eMR_1

(C) MR_2abMR_1

(D) MR_2aMR_2

(E) MR_1bMR_1

58. Game theory is best suited to analyze the pricing behavior of

(A) pure monopolists

(B) pure competitors

(C) monopolistic competitors

(D) oligopolists

(E) monopsonists

59. Game theory can be used to demonstrate that oligopolists

(A) rarely have a price leader present in the industry

(B) rarely consider the potential reactions of rivals

(C) experience economies of scale

(D) can increase their profits through collusion

(E) may be either homogeneous or differentiated

Use the following price strategy matrix to answer **Questions 60–65**.

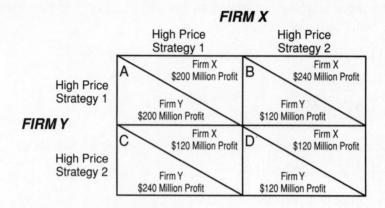

60. If both firms follow a high-price strategy, then

   (A) firm X will realize a $200 million profit and firm Y a $120 million profit

   (B) firm X will realize a $120 million profit and firm Y a $240 million profit

   (C) firm X will realize a $240 million profit and firm Y a $120 million profit

   (D) each will break even for a normal profit

   (E) each will realize a $200 million dollar profit

61. If firm X commits to a low-price strategy and firm Y does not alter its high-price strategy, the most likely result is that

   (A) firm Y will maintain a profit of $200 million, and firm Y will gain market share and $240 million

   (B) firm Y will see a profit of $120 million, and firm X's profits will increase to $240 million

   (C) firm Y will realize $120 million, and firm X $120 million in profits

   (D) firm X will have to return to the high-price strategy if firm Y does not lower its prices

   (E) firm Y will select to match the low-price strategy and see its profits increase to $120 million

62. With independent pricing and a duopoly in place, the noncooperative equilibrium outcome is depicted in which quadrant?

    (A) A

    (B) B

    (C) C

    (D) D

    (E) B and C

63. If the firms engage in price collusion, the equilibrium outcome is depicted in which quadrant?

    (A) A

    (B) B

    (C) C

    (D) D

    (E) C and D

64. The outcome referred to in Question 63 is an example of a dominant strategy because

    (A) both firms face the same incentives

    (B) it is each firm's best action regardless of what the other firm does

    (C) the payoffs are structured so that both firms have a dominant strategy

    (D) the firms are not able to collude

    (E) of all the conditions stated in (A) through (D).

65. If the firms collude, the temptation to cheat on that agreement is great because

    (A) firm X can increase its profits by lowering its price

    (B) firm X can raise its profits further by increasing its price

    (C) firm X can raise its profits by decreasing its production costs

    (D) firm Y can raise its profits by decreasing its production costs

    (E) greater profits would result from both firms charging a lower price

66. Suppose an oligopolist assumes its rivals will ignore a price increase but match a price cut. The oligopolist assumes this because the

    (A) demand curve has a constant negative slope

    (B) supply curve has a constant positive slope

    (C) demand curve lies below its marginal revenue curve

    (D) demand curve is kinked above the equilibrium price to match its competitor's demand curve

    (E) demand curve is kinked below the equilibrium price to match its competitor's demand curve

67. The data in the following table provide the government with the outcomes of the public highway infrastructure. On the basis of cost-benefit analysis, what should the government undertake?

Highway Plan	Total Cost (in millions)	Total Benefit (in millions)
A (one lane)	$10	$16
B (two lanes)	$24	$36
C (three lanes)	$44	$52
D (four lanes)	$72	$64
E (five lanes)	$100	$74

    (A) Plan E   (D) Plan B

    (B) Plan D   (E) Plan A

    (C) Plan C

68. A sales tax is a regressive tax because the

    (A) percentage of income paid as taxes falls as income rises

    (B) percentage of income paid as taxes rises as income rises

    (C) administrative costs associated with the collection of the tax are relatively high

    (D) percentage of income paid as taxes is constant as income rises

    (E) tax tends to reduce the total volume of consumption expenditures

Use the following graph to answer **Questions 69–70**.

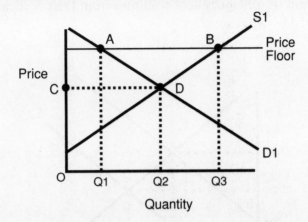

69. The government imposes the price floor on the dairy industry because of the positive externalities of drinking milk. What is the most likely outcome of this intervention?

   (A) The price of milk falls.

   (B) The quantity of milk consumed rises sharply.

   (C) The quantity supplied at point A is less than the quantity demanded, and a shortage results.

   (D) A surplus of milk (area Q_1ABQ_3) results.

   (E) A shortage of milk (area Q_1ABQ_3) results.

70. If the government places a tax on milk instead of a price floor, the outcome changes because

   (A) the price of milk falls by the amount of the tax

   (B) the quantity of milk reflects the positive externalities mentioned in Question 69

   (C) no surplus of milk results

   (D) the demand for milk decreases

   (E) the supply of milk increases and the price to consumers falls

71. The tax discussed in Question 70 is depicted in the following model. The amount of efficiency loss resulting from the tax (dead weight) is represented by what area?

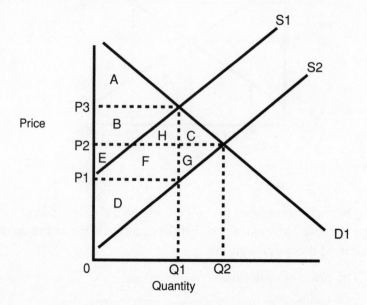

(A) C + G

(B) D + F + H + C + G

(C) A + B + E

(D) 0 + P1 + Q1

(E) 0 + P2 + Q2

72. A society that wishes to achieve greater income equality is most likely to have which of the following?

(A) A regressive income tax system

(B) A regressive income tax system, low estate taxes, and high sales taxes

(C) A progressive income tax system and high estate and gift taxes

(D) A progressive income tax system and low estate and gift taxes

(E) A proportional income tax system

73. Normal profit is

    (A) a cost, because any excess of total receipts over total costs goes to the business owner

    (B) an external explicit cost

    (C) a cost, because it represents payments made for the resources the business owner owns and supplies in his or her enterprise

    (D) not a cost, because a firm can avoid this payment by temporarily closing down

    (E) not a cost of production, because it need not be realized for a firm to retain entrepreneurial ability

74. A firm's economic profit is

    (A) the result of greed and is the cause of social inequality

    (B) usually lower than its normal profit

    (C) profit above that which the firm needs to compensate for the time and other resources the owner supplies to the business

    (D) a cost of production

    (E) a signal to the firm that it is producing too much output

75. From society's point of view, the economic function of profit and loss is to

    (A) promote the equal distribution of real assets and wealth

    (B) achieve full employment and price-level stability

    (C) contribute to a more equal distribution of income

    (D) reward the lucky and punish the hard working

    (E) reallocate resources from less desired to more desired uses

Use the following table to answer **Questions 76–78**.

The table describes the production relationship for firm XYZ. Assume that this firm can hire as many workers as it wants for $75 per day and can sell all its output for $5 each.

Workers	Total Output (units)
3	60
4	80
5	105
6	125
7	140
8	150

76. In what type of environment does firm XYZ operate?

    (A) Monopsony

    (B) Perfectly competitive

    (C) Not enough information to determine

    (D) Imperfectly competitive

    (E) Monopolistically competitive

77. How many workers will firm XYZ hire?

    (A) 3   (D) 6

    (B) 4   (E) 7

    (C) 5

78. If the wage rate at which the firm can hire workers increases to $120 per day and the selling price of shirts increases to $6 each, how many workers can firm XYZ hire?

    (A) 3   (D) 6

    (B) 4   (E) 7

    (C) 5

Use the following table to answer **Questions 79–80**.

The table describes the production costs for firm Z.

Output Quantity	Average Fixed Costs	Average Variable Costs	Marginal Costs
0			
1	100.00	55.00	55.00
2	50.00	45.00	35.00
3	33.33	50.00	60.00
4	25.00	55.00	70.00
5	20.00	60.00	80.00
6	16.67	65.00	90.00

79. The average total cost to firm Z for 3 units is

(A) $35.00

(B) $83.33

(C) $85.00

(D) $95.00

(E) $100.00

80. If firm Z operates in a perfectly competitive industry and the market price is $75.00, how many units can firm Z sell and what is its total profit or loss?

(A) 4 units and a loss of $20.00

(B) 5 units and a loss of $375.00

(C) 0 units and a loss of $100.00

(D) 2 units and a profit per unit of $40.00

(E) 4 units and a profit per unit of $20.00

CLEP MICROECONOMICS
PRACTICE TEST 2

ANSWER KEY

1. (A)	28. (B)	55. (A)
2. (D)	29. (E)	56. (B)
3. (E)	30. (A)	57. (C)
4. (A)	31. (A)	58. (D)
5. (B)	32. (E)	59. (D)
6. (A)	33. (A)	60. (E)
7. (E)	34. (C)	61. (B)
8. (E)	35. (C)	62. (D)
9. (E)	36. (E)	63. (A)
10. (A)	37. (D)	64. (E)
11. (A)	38. (B)	65. (A)
12. (D)	39. (D)	66. (E)
13. (C)	40. (C)	67. (D)
14. (B)	41. (D)	68. (A)
15. (B)	42. (D)	69. (D)
16. (D)	43. (A)	70. (C)
17. (C)	44. (E)	71. (A)
18. (E)	45. (C)	72. (C)
19. (A)	46. (D)	73. (C)
20. (D)	47. (D)	74. (C)
21. (B)	48. (C)	75. (E)
22. (C)	49. (D)	76. (B)
23. (A)	50. (D)	77. (E)
24. (B)	51. (A)	78. (D)
25. (A)	52. (B)	79. (B)
26. (D)	53. (B)	80. (A)
27. (A)	54. (E)	

DETAILED EXPLANATIONS OF ANSWERS

PRACTICE TEST 2

1.   **(A)**   This is the definition of scarcity and the basic premise of economics.

2.   **(D)**   A production possibilities frontier curve allows the economist to see the various combinations of goods that the same resource inputs can produce. All combinations are of equal efficiency, so no one choice is preferred relative to another.

3.   **(E)**   This question further illustrates the concept of efficient use of resources and shows that an economy has limits to what it is capable of producing in the short run and can underproduce as well.

4.   **(A)**   This question illustrates the law of diminishing returns. All resource inputs (i.e., labor) are not equal and as such are less productive as more are employed. As a firm adds more workers, at some point, the total output falls as the least productive workers are added.

5.   **(B)**   The marginal cost curve illustrates the impact of diminishing returns on the cost of production. In other words, as more resources are used, their productive output decreases at an increasing rate. This means that at some point (when minimum economy of scale is reached) as the producer's output increases, the cost of production rises because inputs are less productive.

6.   **(A)**   Determining comparative advantage (the basis for specialization and ensuing trade) is seeking the least cost of production. In this case the cost to Obiwan of 1 page of reading is 50 words typing (50/1 = 50 to 1), whereas to Anikan the cost of 1 page of reading is only 20 words of typing (60/3 = 20 to 1). So the most productive combination is to let Obiwan type and Anikan read.

7.   **(E)**   An economist wants to determine consumers' overall response to a price change to predict their behavior. Producers value predictions of consumer behavior because they can predict how their revenues or profits will change as they raise or lower their market prices.

8.   **(E)**   The percentage of change in the quantity demanded is (60 – 50)/50 = 0.20, and the percentage of change in price is ($100 – $90)/100 = 0.10. Because 0.20/0.10 = 2, demand is elastic. Remember, a coefficient less than 1 indicates inelasticity and a coefficient greater than 1 indicates elasticity for both demand and supply.

9.   **(E)**   The total-revenue test reveals that the upper portion of a demand curve is more elastic than the lower portion, meaning that any decrease in price will cause total revenue to increase. Lowering the price from $8 to $7 increases the total revenue from $8 (1 unit × $8) to $14 (2 units × $7). This gives the firm further insight into what portion of the demand curve it should operate in given the choice.

10.   **(A)**   This is the total-revenue test for elasticity. If a firm is in the inelastic portion of its demand curve, a decrease in output accompanied by a decrease in quantity demanded at a higher price causes total revenue to increase.

11.   **(A)**   The inelastic portion of a demand curve is defined as the result of an increase in output accompanied by a decrease in price that results in a decline in total revenue.

12.   **(D)**   This is the law of diminishing marginal utility. It is what causes the downward slope to a consumer demand curve.

13.   **(C)**   Marginal utility is the change in total utility divided by the change in quantity. Therefore, because the total utility of the first two units is 30 (18 + 12) and the total utility of all three is 39, the marginal utility is 9 (39 – 30).

14.   **(B)**   This assumption allows the economist to predict consumer behavior to a market that is in dynamic interaction with supply.

15.   **(B)**   This is a simple restatement of the utility-maximizing rule on which question 14 is based. Consumers will spend their income in such a way that they derive the greatest satisfaction possible from each dollar spent. To do otherwise would be irrational because the consumer's money would be poorly spent if good X costs the same as good Y and has the same

utility but the consumer buys more of good X. The satisfaction from good X would have decreased to less than the satisfaction of Y.

16. **(D)**   This is a test of the formula used to maximize consumer utility per dollar spent. As the consumer buys more of good X, its marginal utility falls (remember the law of diminishing marginal utility), so the ratio of marginal utility to dollars gets closer to 1. As the consumer buys less of good Y, its marginal utility increases, raising its ratio of marginal utility per dollar. Either approach works to balance the equation.

17. **(C)**   The formula $MU_X/P_X = MU_Y/P_Y = \$52$ allows you to derive the utility-maximizing combination of goods equal to a budget limit. At 4 units of product X, $MU_X/P_X = 24/\$8 = 3/1$ ($32 spent), and at 5 units of product Y, $MU_Y/P_Y = 12/\$4 = 3/1$ ($20 spent). The final equation ratio is $3/1 = 3/1 = \$52$ budget limit.

18. **(E)**   The formula given in explanation 17 still applies, but the higher budget allows the consumer to purchase more of each item, lowering the marginal utility until they are obtaining 1 marginal unit for each dollar spent. At 7 units of product X and 7 units of product Y, the equation yields $8/8 = 4/4 = \$84$ $[(7 \times 8) + (7 \times 4) = \$84]$.

19. **(A)**   The firm has not reached normal profit because the $10 price it receives is less than its average total cost of $11. However, because its average variable cost of $9 is exceeded, it can continue to operate. It would choose to do so in the short run because other firms that are less cost-efficient exit the industry, and the resulting supply decrease causes the price to rise and normal profit to return in the long run.

20. **(D)**   When an industry is experiencing a loss, firms exit because the supply for the industry is reduced; as a result, the long-run normal profit level is attained.

21. **(B)**   Diseconomies of scale reflect the fact that at high output levels, firms incur higher costs because labor becomes less productive. For example, very large firms have a bureaucracy that slows decision making, and time is money.

22. **(C)**   Economies of scale reflect the law of diminishing returns. Initially, resource input specialization results in increasing output from additional inputs. As output increases relative to inputs, the firm gets more product from fewer workers, thus its average total cost falls.

23. **(A)** Constant return to efficiency simply means that at both low output levels and high output levels, costs are the same. This is the basis for monopolistically competitive firms being both small and large in output. Because small firms and large firms have the same costs, they are competitive in the marketplace.

24. **(B)** This model depicts the long-run average total cost curve for an oligopoly. It reflects a large economy of scale that serves as a barrier to entry, because a new firm must produce at a high output to attain the minimum cost per unit. This discourages competition because the capital risk is high relative to reward.

25. **(A)** The main point of this model is to show that efficiencies of scale and diseconomies of scale occur at low levels of output. Only small producers with ease of entry and exit can exist in this very competitive space.

26. **(D)** As the demand for a good decreases, the equilibrium price falls. This lower price covers the costs of fewer firms, so the quantity supplied decreases. Those producers with costs lower than the equilibrium price are called "producer surplus" by economists.

27. **(A)** This is an example of one of the determinants of demand. If the price of a good increases and a substitute is available, the demand for the substitute increases. This shift in demand increases the equilibrium price and quantity of the substitute good.

28. **(B)** As the supply of a good decreases, the equilibrium price rises. The higher price reduces the number of consumers whose utility is covered by the higher price, so the quantity demanded decreases. Consumers whose high level of satisfaction allows them to pay the higher equilibrium price are called "consumer surplus" by economists.

29. **(E)** This is the graphic portrayal of explanation 26.

30. **(A)** Pure public goods are not divisible and are not exclusionary. A public beach cannot be divided into individually owned lots, and it is open to all beachgoers because the price of entrance does not prevent usage.

31. **(A)** If a firm's costs fall and its price remains constant, output increases because greater profit occurs at higher output levels. The supply curve shifts to the right.

32. **(E)** As the monopolist sells more output, the quantity demanded requires that a lower price be present (the monopolist has a downward-sloping demand curve). Thus total revenue increases at a decreasing rate, making marginal revenue lie inside the demand curve (D > MR). A purely competitive firm, on the other hand, takes the price dictated by the industry so it can sell everything it makes at a constant industry price. This makes the demand curve perfectly elastic, and because there is a constant rate of change in the total revenue, it is equal to the demand, which in turn is equal to price (P = D = MR).

33. **(A)** Because firms have ease of entrance and exit, when economic profit is present they enter, and when economic loss is present they exit. The result is that in the long run, when P = Minimum ATC firms have no incentive to enter or exit the industry, and normal profit results.

34. **(C)** New firms will be attracted by the economic profit, causing the industry supply to increase, prices to fall, and normal profit to result in the long run.

35. **(C)** MR = MC at 5 units. The firm would set the price at $14 and obtain its maximum economic profit under these market conditions.

36. **(E)** The monopoly makes the price by determining the output quantity relative to the demand for the good. It does not have the power to dictate price, because the demand of the consumer is still relevant.

37. **(D)** The price-discriminating, imperfectly competitive firm raises the price for each additional unit it sells. It can capture higher total revenue because it operates in the elastic portion of its demand curve.

38. **(B)** Negative externalities are costs borne by those not involved in the production or consumption of the good and as such are not reflected in the market price of the good. As a result, the output is greater and the price lower than it would be if the true cost to society were reflected in the price.

39. **(D)** A subsidy is a societal price support that reflects the positive impact that increased consumption of the good has on society as a whole (like education). A reduction of a subsidy to the consumer decreases overall demand.

40. **(C)** Equilibrium occurs where S = MRP (or demand).

41. **(D)** The monopsonist pays below equilibrium by underemploying the labor force.

42. **(D)** Monopsonists operate where MRP = MRC. They then under-employ (100), pay down to the S curve ($2.50), and profit from the MRP of $7.50.

43. **(A)** When firms merge they add market share. Thus their total revenue increases, and they can reduce costs because they can eliminate duplicate labor and capital, increasing output efficiency and lowering average total cost. This is often termed synergy by merging firms.

44. **(E)** At the lower wage the quantity demanded by firms increases.

45. **(C)** A price floor below equilibrium causes a shortage of minimum wage workers because the quantity demanded greatly surpasses the quantity of workers supplied.

46. **(D)** The industry supply has shifted right from S_1 to S_2. This demonstrates an increase in supply. At S_1 the industry and firm price is such that economic profit is present. By definition a purely competitive industry has ease of entrance and exit, so firms attracted by the profit enter the industry.

47. **(D)** As discussed in explanation 46, at S_1 the industry price is above the ATC curve, indicating that the firm is in economic profit, not normal profit.

48. **(C)** This illustrates the definition of an inferior good and its relationship to consumer income.

49. **(D)** These are key characteristics of monopolistically competitive firms.

50. **(D)** Product differentiation enables the firm to have some pricing power. Because the monopoly features a unique product, its control of output is the basis for its pricing power.

51. **(A)** The profit-maximizing formula of MR = MC applies, and the demand curve determines the market price.

52. **(B)** This is the output based on the profit-maximizing formula.

53. **(B)** In the long-run, demand is at D_1 because normal profit is the best the firm can do. If the firm were enjoying demand D, then other firms, attracted by the economic profits, would enter the industry until normal profit was attained.

54. **(E)** An import tax on steel would increase the price of foreign steel. This would shift the total supply of steel leftward and raise its price. Domestic costs would not change, but the market price would increase, making products that use steel cost more to make.

55. **(A)** Should the price move lower, D_2 will have no choice but to match that price or lose market share to D_1. This forms the kinked demand curve for D_2.

56. **(B)** Firm D2 has no choice but to match Firm D1 should it lower its price below equilibrium e. If it does not match the lower price it will lose customers to Firm D1. This situation is typical of oligopolies and explains why prices tend to remain stable, as firms prefer not to engage in price wars.

57. **(C)** Just as the demand curve kinks at equilibrium, so too does the marginal revenue curve because it reflects the new change in total revenue.

58. **(D)** Game theory is a pricing strategy employed by a few large firms that have significant barriers to entry. If it were easy for firms to enter or exit, any firm would have so little pricing power as to render output limits useless in the long run.

59. **(D)** Collusion is price fixing and as such empowers firms to extract the greatest possible profit from a market. It allows a firm to behave as a monopoly and "price make."

60. **(E)** The high-price strategy, quadrant A, shows the profit outcome of both firms.

61. **(B)** If firm Y does not match the low-price strategy of firm X, then firm X takes market share from firm Y and increases its profits. This is why firms in oligopoly tend to follow a price cut and engage in "price wars."

62. **(D)** Noncooperative equilibrium (part of Nobel Prize-winning mathematician John Nash's game theory) is the outcome that results from each firm acting only on what it sees as its best course of action, ignoring the ef-

fects that this action has on the other firm. So firm X pursues the low-price strategy, seeking the $240 million profit, unaware that firm Y has responded in kind, thus leaving both firms with the $120 million profit.

63. **(A)** Firms would realize that if both follow the high-price strategy, they both enjoy the highest profit possible and create a very stable market share environment. Repeated interaction of firms can result in the same outcome event, although no formal collusion takes place. This is why an oligopoly rarely changes its pricing strategy.

64. **(E)** This question allows you to review the conditions in oligopoly that define a dominant strategy.

65. **(A)** This question shows why so often, even when contractual agreements are in place, a firm will "cheat," because a lower price allows it to steal market share and increase total profits. OPEC is a prime historical example of firms in collusion operating "under the table" for these reasons.

66. **(E)** This kink in the demand curve represents the reason that competitors in a price war must match the lower price or lose market share to the firm whose demand curve lies within its rival's.

67. **(D)** Plan B is the best government selection because the cost of $24 million relative to the benefit of $36 million results in a net benefit to society of $12 million. Plans D and E represent overallocation of resources, and plans A and B represent relative underallocation.

68. **(A)** Under a regressive tax, people with low incomes pay a higher percentage than do those with high incomes. For example, a $1 tax to a person earning $10 is a higher percentage (10%) of income than that $1 tax is to a person earning $100 (1%).

69. **(D)** A surplus of milk occurs because the quantity demanded (A) is less than the quantity supplied (B).

70. **(C)** A tax on milk shifts the supply curve left, and the new equilibrium results in a higher price and lower quantity. However, no shortage or surplus occurs because all the milk brought to market sells.

71. **(A)** The loss of efficiency refers to the higher price and lower quantity available in the market after the tax; thus the loss is C + G.

72. **(C)**   A progressive tax allows for a higher percentage of tax as personal income increases, an estate tax prevents inheritance of assets from being a source of higher income, and a gift tax prevents the wealthy from giving their assets away. By imposing the three taxes, the government effects a transfer from the "haves" to the "have nots."

73. **(C)**   Normal profit is how the economist accounts for the value sacrificed to start and run a business, like capital and entrepreneurial skill.

74. **(C)**   Economic profit is any revenue greater than normal profit or a normal rate of return.

75. **(E)**   This is Adam Smith's "invisible hand" at work. The free-market system employs prices as a signal of change in costs or utility of goods or services and accounts for the speed at which the market adapts to change.

76. **(B)**   Firm XYZ operates in a perfectly competitive environment because it hires as many workers as it wants at an industry wage and can sell all it makes at a constant industry price.

77. **(E)**   The firm will hire seven workers because the MRP of the seventh worker is $75, which is equal to the MRC of $75. For the seventh worker, 140 total units $\times$ $5 = $700 in total revenue, whereas for the sixth worker, 125 total units $\times$ $5 = $625 in total revenue; thus the change in total revenue is $75, which is equal to the $75 change in total cost. The formula used to determine the behavior of profit-maximizing firms is MRP = MRC.

78. **(D)**   The firm will hire six workers because the MRP of the sixth worker is $120, which is equal to the MRC of $120. For the sixth worker, 125 total units $\times$ $6 = $750, whereas for the fifth worker, 105 total units $\times$ $6 = $630; thus the change in total revenue is $120, which is equal to the $120 change in total cost of one more worker.

79. **(B)**   ATC = AFC + AVC. So the third unit of output has an ATC of $83.33 ($33.33 + $50.00).

80. **(A)**   This firm has an economic loss because its price, marginal return, and demand are all equal and below the ATC curve. It still operates where MR = MC because that is its least loss level of output. Since this firm is covering its AVC, it continues operating in the short run because firms may leave the industry, prices rise, and profits return.

GLOSSARY

aggregate demand—shows the total quantity of goods and services consumed at different price and output levels.

aggregate demand/aggregate supply (AD/AS) model—uses aggregate demand and aggregate supply to determine and explain price level, real domestic output, disposable income, and employment.

aggregate expenditure—all spending for final goods and services in an economy: $C + I_g + G + Xn = AE$.

aggregate supply shocks—unexpected, large changes in resource costs that shift an economy's aggregate supply curve.

allocative efficiency—distribution of resources among firms and industries to obtain production quantities of the products most wanted by society (consumers); where marginal cost equals marginal benefit.

appreciation (of the dollar)—an increase in the value of the dollar relative to the currency of another nation, so that a dollar buys more of the foreign currency and thus foreign goods become cheaper; critical to long-run trade equilibrium.

asset—items of monetary value owned by a firm or individual; opposite is liability.

asset demand for money—various amounts of money people want to hold as a store of value; the amount varies inversely with the interest rate; critical to monetary policy.

average fixed cost (AFC)—firm's total fixed cost divided by output.

average product—total output produced per unit of a resource employed (total product divided by the quantity of input).

average total cost (ATC)—firm's total cost divided by output, equal to average fixed cost plus average variable cost (AFC + AVC = ATC).

average variable cost (AVC)—firm's total variable cost divided by output.

balanced-budget multiplier—extent to which an equal change in government spending and taxes changes equilibrium gross domestic product; always has a value of 1, because it is equal to the amount of the equal changes in G and T (T is subject to the MPS of consumers and spending is not).

balance of payments account—the summary of a nation's current account and its financial account.

balance of trade—is a nation's current account balance, net exports.

balance sheet—statement of the assets and liabilities that determines a firm's net (solvency).

barrier to entry—artificial prevention of the entry of firms into an industry.

Board of Governors—seven-member group that supervises and controls the money and banking system; appointed by president to 14-year staggered terms; the Federal Reserve Board.

bond—financial instrument through which a borrower (corporate or government) is contracted to pay the principal at a specified interest rate at a specific date (maturity) in the future; promissory note.

break-even point—output at which a (competitive) firm's total cost and total revenue are equal (TR = TC); an output at which a firm has neither an economic profit nor a loss, at which it earns only a normal profit.

Bretton Woods system—international monetary system developed after the Second World War. Under this system, adjustable pegs were employed, the International Monetary Fund helped stabilize foreign exchange rates, and gold (gold standard set at \$35 U.S. per ounce of gold) and the dollar were used as international monetary reserves.

budget deficit—amount by which the spending of the (federal) government exceeds its tax revenues in any year.

budget surplus—amount by which the tax revenues of the (federal) government exceed its spending in any year.

built-in (automatic) stabilizers—programs that react to changes in the business cycle without additional government action, increasing government's budget deficit (or reducing its surplus) during a recession and increasing government's budget surplus (or reducing its deficit) during inflation. Unemployment insurance is one such program.

business cycle—records the increases and decreases in the level of economic activity over periods of time. Consists of expansion (boom), peak, recession (bust or contraction), trough (bottom), and recovery phases. GDP data is generally used to plot this cycle, a lagging indicator.

capital—resources (buildings, machinery, and equipment) used to produce goods and services; also called investment goods.

capital account—section of a nation's international balance-of-payments balance sheet that records foreign purchases of U.S. assets (money in) and U.S. purchases of foreign assets (money out).

capital account inflow (outflow)—reflects the net difference between foreign funds invested in the home country minus the domestic funds invested in the foreign country. A component of the balance of payments account.

capitalism—free market economic system in which property is privately owned and the invisible forces of supply and demand set price and quantity.

cartel—overt agreement among firms (or countries) in an industry to fix the price of a product and establish output quotas.

central bank—government agency whose chief function is the control of the nation's money supply; the Federal Reserve.

change in demand—change in the quantity demanded of a good or service at all prices; a shift of the demand curve to the left (decrease) or right (increase).

change in supply—change in the quantity supplied of a good or service at all prices; a shift of the supply curve to the left (decrease) or right (increase).

circular flow model—flow of resource inputs from households to businesses and of g/s from businesses to households. A flow in the opposite direction of money—businesses to households for inputs and from households to businesses for g/s—occurs simultaneously.

Classical economics—school of macroeconomic generalizations accepted by most economists prior to the depression of the 1930s; a main feature was that the free market economy was self-regulating and would naturally return to full employment levels of output.

collusion—when firms act together (collude) to fix prices, divide a market, or otherwise restrict competition; illegal in the United States.

command system—economic system in which property is publicly owned (means of production) and government uses central economic planning to direct and coordinate economic activities; state-planned economy in which price and quantity are set by government (as in the former USSR).

comparative advantage—determines specialization and exchange rate for trade between nations; based on the nation with the lower relative or comparative cost of production.

competition—Adam Smith's requirement for success of a free market, a market of independent buyers and sellers competing with one another; includes ease of access to and exit from the marketplace.

complementary goods—goods that are used together, so if the price of one falls, the demand for the other decreases as well (and vice versa).

concentration ratio—a simple method of determining a monopoly, which adds the percentage of the total sales of an industry made by the four largest sellers in the industry. If the sum is greater than 50%, the industry is considered a shared monopoly.

conglomerate merger—merger of a firm in one industry with a firm in an unrelated industry.

consumer price index (CPI)—index that measures the prices of a set "basket" of some 300 g/s bought by a "typical" consumer; used by government as a main indicator of the rate of inflation.

consumer surplus—that portion of the demand curve that lies above the equilibrium price level and denotes those consumers that would be willing to buy the g/s at higher price levels.

contractionary fiscal policy—combination of government reduction in spending and a net increase in taxes, for the purpose of decreasing aggregate demand, lowering price levels, and thus controlling inflation.

corporation—legal entity ("like a person") chartered by a state or the federal government; limits liability for business debt to the assets of the firm.

cost-push inflation—when an increase in resource costs shifts the aggregate supply curve inward, resulting in an increase in the price level and unemployment; also termed *stagflation*.

cross elasticity of demand—ratio of the percentage change in quantity demanded of one good to the percentage change in the price of another good. If the coefficient is positive, the two goods are substitute. If the coefficient is negative, they are considered complementary.

crowding-out effect—caused by the federal government's increased borrowing in the money market that results in a rise in interest rates. The rise in interest rates results in a decrease in gross business domestic investment (I_g), which reduces the effectiveness of expansionary fiscal policy.

currency rate of exchange—the price in one domestic currency to purchase a unit of another nation's currency. For example, 1 U.S. dollar buys 1.50 Canadian dollars.

current account—section in a nation's international balance of payments that records its exports and imports of goods and services, its net investment income, and its net transfers. A component of the balance of payments account.

cyclical deficit—a government budget deficit caused by a recession and the resultant decline in tax revenues.

cyclical unemployment—type of unemployment caused by recession; less than full employment aggregate demand.

deadweight loss (efficiency loss)—the foregone total societal surplus associated with the levy of a tax that discourages what had heretofore been a mutually advantageous market transaction.

deflation—decline in the economy's price level; indicates contraction in business cycle or may signal expansion of total output (aggregate supply moves to the right).

demand—the quantity of a g/s that buyers wish to buy at various prices.

depreciation (of the dollar)—decrease in the value of the dollar relative to another currency, so that the dollar buys a smaller amount of the foreign currency and therefore the price of foreign goods increases; tends to reduce imports and increase exports.

derived demand—orders for a production input that depend on a demand for the product that the input helps to produce.

determinants of demand—factors other than price that alter (shift) the quantities demanded of a good or service.

determinants of supply—factors other than price that alter (shift) the quantities supplied of a good or service.

direct relationship—correlation between two variables that change in the same direction; for example, income and spending.

discount rate—interest rate that the Federal Reserve Banks charge on the loans they make to banks (different from the federal funds rate).

discretionary fiscal policy—deliberate changes in taxes (rates and types) and government spending by Congress.

disposable income—personal income minus personal taxes; income available for consumption expenditures and saving.

dissaving—when spending for consumer g/s exceeds disposable income.

dumping—predatory business practice; sale of products below cost in a foreign country or below the domestic prices.

durable good—consumer good with an expected life (use) of three or more years; decrease in sales indicates recession, as contraction affects these goods before nondurables.

easy money policy—Federal Reserve actions designed to stimulate gross business domestic investment (I_g) and thus aggregate demand; counters recession by increasing the money supply to lower interest rates and expand real GDP.

economic efficiency—use of the minimum necessary inputs to obtain the most societally beneficial quantity of g/s; employs both productive and allocative efficiency.

economic profit—total revenue of a firm minus its economic costs (both explicit and implicit costs); also termed *pure profit* and *above-normal profit*.

economic rent—price paid for the use of land and other natural resources, the supply of which is fixed.

economies of scale—savings in the average total cost of production as the firm expands the size of plant (its output) in the long run.

elastic demand—product or resource demand whose price elasticity is greater than 1. This means that the resulting percentage change in quantity demanded is greater than the percentage change in price.

elastic supply—product or resource supply whose price elasticity is greater than 1. This means that the resulting percentage change in quantity supplied is greater than the percentage change in price.

entitlement programs—government programs, such as social insurance, food stamps, Medicare, and Medicaid, that guarantee benefits to all who fit the programs' criteria.

equilibrium price—price at which the quantity demanded and the quantity supplied are equal (intersect), shelves clear, and price stability occurs.

equilibrium quantity—quantity demanded and supplied at the equilibrium price.

excess capacity—plant resources underused when imperfectly competitive firms produce less output than that associated with achieving minimum average total cost.

exchange rate—trade ratio of one nation's currency for another nation's currency.

expansionary fiscal policy—combination of government increases in spending and a net decrease in taxes, for the purpose of increasing aggregate demand, increasing output and disposable income, and lowering unemployment.

expected rate of return—profit a firm anticipates it will obtain by purchasing capital goods; influences investment demand for money.

explicit cost—payment a firm must make to an outsider to obtain a production input.

factors of production—resources: land, capital, and entrepreneurial ability.

federal funds rate—the interest rate banks and other depository institutions charge one another on overnight loans made out of their excess reserves; targeted by monetary policy.

Federal Open Market Committee (FOMC)—the 12-member group that determines the purchase and sale policies of the Federal Reserve Banks in the market for U.S. government securities; affects federal funds rate.

Federal Reserve Banks—12 banks chartered by the U.S. government to control the money supply and perform other functions such as clearing checks.

Federal Trade Commission (FTC)—commission of five members established by the Federal Trade Commission Act of 1914 to investigate unfair competitive practices of firms, to hold hearings on complaints of such practices, and to issue cease-and-desist orders when firms have been found to have engaged in such practices.

financial account (capital account)—the difference between a country's sale of assets to foreigners and its purchase of foreign assets. A component of the balance of payments.

fixed cost—any cost that remains constant when the firm changes its output.

fixed exchange rate—rate of currency exchange that is set, prevented from rising or falling with changes in currency supply and demand; opposite of floating rate.

floating exchange rate—rate of exchange determined by the international demand for and supply of a nation's money; free to increase or decrease.

frictional unemployment—unemployment caused by workers' voluntarily changing jobs or workers' being between jobs.

full employment unemployment rate—natural rate of unemployment when there is no cyclical unemployment. In the United States, equals between 4% and 5%, because some frictional and structural unemployment is unavoidable.

GDP deflator—price index found by dividing nominal GDP by real GDP; used to adjust nominal GDP to real GDP.

General Agreement on Tariffs and Trade (GATT)—international agreement, reached in 1947, in which 23 nations agreed to reduce tariff rates and eliminate import quotas. The Uruguay Round of the GATT talks led to the World Trade Organization.

government transfer payment—money (or g/s) issued to an individual by a government for which the government receives no direct payment from that person.

gross domestic product (GDP)—total market value of all final goods and services produced annually within the boundaries of the United States, whether by U.S. or foreign-supplied resources.

horizontal merger—merger into a single firm of two firms that produce the same product and sell it in the same geographic market.

hyperinflation—a very rapid rise in the price level; an extremely high rate of inflation.

imperfect competition—all market structures except pure competition; includes monopoly, monopolistic competition, and oligopoly.

implicit cost—the monetary income a firm sacrifices when it uses a resource it owns rather than supplying the resource in the market; equal to what the resource could have earned in the best-paying alternative employment; includes a normal profit.

indifference curve—curve showing the different combinations of two products that yield the same satisfaction or utility to a consumer.

inelastic demand—product or resource demand for which the elasticity coefficient for price is less than 1. This means the resulting percentage change in quantity demanded is less than the percentage change in price.

inelastic supply—product or resource supply for which the price elasticity coefficient is less than 1. The percentage change in quantity supplied is less than the percentage change in price.

inferior good—a g/s the consumption of which declines as income rises (and vice versa), with price remaining constant.

inflation—rise in the general level of prices.

inflation (rational) expectations—a key determinant that impacts the loanable funds market for both borrowers and lenders.

inflation targeting—a central bank practice that requires a predetermined, agreed upon rate of inflation to be sought by monetary policy.

inflationary gap—amount by which the aggregate expenditure and schedule must shift downward to decrease the nominal GDP to its full employment noninflationary level.

injection—a way of viewing an increase of a component(s) of aggregate expenditure that may result in an overall increase of aggregate demand; opposite of leakage. Addition of spending such as investment, government purchases, or net exports.

interest—payment for the use of borrowed money.

intermediate goods—products purchased for resale or further processing or manufacturing.

international balance of payments—all the transactions that took place between one nation and those of all other nations during a year.

International Monetary Fund (IMF)—the international association of nations that was formed after the Second World War to make loans of foreign monies to nations with temporary payment deficits and, until the early 1970s, to administer the adjustable pegs. It now mainly makes loans to nations that face possible defaults on private and government loans.

inventories—goods that have been produced but remain unsold.

inverse relationship—the relationship between two variables that change in opposite directions; for example, product price and quantity demanded.

invisible hand—tendency of firms and resource suppliers that seek to further their own self-interests in competitive markets also to promote the interest of society as a whole.

Keynesian economics—macroeconomic generalizations leading to the conclusion that a capitalistic economy is characterized by macroeconomic instability and that fiscal policy and monetary policy can be used to promote full employment, price level stability, and economic growth.

kinked demand curve—demand curve for a noncollusive oligopolist, which is based on the assumption that rivals will follow a price decrease and ignore a price increase.

Laffer Curve—curve relating government tax rates and tax revenues and on which a particular tax rate (between 0 and 100 percent) maximizes tax revenues.

law of demand—the principle that, other things being equal, an increase in the price of a product will reduce the quantity of that product demanded, and conversely for a decrease in price.

law of diminishing marginal utility—the principle that as a consumer increases the consumption of a good or service, the marginal utility obtained from each additional unit of the g/s decreases.

law of diminishing returns—the principle that as successive increments of a variable resource are added to a fixed resource, the marginal product of the variable resource will eventually decrease.

law of increasing opportunity costs—the principle that as the production of a good increases, the opportunity cost of producing an additional unit rises.

law of supply—the principle that, other things being equal, an increase in the price of a product will increase the quantity of that product supplied, and conversely for a price decrease.

leakage—(1) a withdrawal of potential spending from the income-expenditures stream via saving, tax payments, or imports; (2) a withdrawal that reduces the lending potential of the banking system.

least-cost combination of resources—the quantity of each resource a firm must employ to produce a particular output at the lowest total cost; the combination at which the ratio of the marginal product of a resource to its marginal resource cost (to its price if the resource is employed in a competitive market) is the same for the last dollar spent on each of the resources employed.

liability—a debt with a monetary value; an amount owed by a firm or an individual.

liquidity—the ease with which an asset can be converted—quickly— into cash with little or no loss of purchasing power. Money is said to be perfectly liquid, whereas other assets have a lesser degree of liquidity.

liquidity trap—a point in an economy where the nominal interest rate is zero and as a result theoretically (there are other ways the "Fed" could inject money into an economy, such as buying paper clips) where monetary policy would be exhausted.

loanable funds market—a conceptual market wherein the demand for money is determined by borrowers and the supply is determined by lenders. Market equilibrium prices the interest rate.

long run—time frame necessary for producers to alter resource inputs and increase or decrease output; time frame necessary for adjustments to be made as a result of shifts in aggregate demand and supply.

Lorenz curve—a model that demonstrates the cumulative percentage of population and their cumulative share of income; used to show shifts in income distribution across population over time.

M1, M2, M3—money supply measurements that increasingly broaden the definition of money measured; critical to monetarism and interest rates.

macroeconomics—the portion of economics concerned with the overall performance of the economy; focused on aggregate demand-aggregate supply relationship, and the resultant output, income, employment, and price levels.

marginal benefit—change in total benefit that results from the consumption of one more unit of output.

marginal cost—change in total cost that results from the sale of one more unit of output.

marginal product—change in total output relative to the change in resource input.

marginal propensity to consume—change in consumption spending relative to a change in income.

marginal propensity to save—change in saving relative to a change in income.

marginal revenue—change in total revenue that results from the sale of one more unit of product.

marginal revenue cost (MRC)—change in total cost with the addition of one more unit of resource input for production.

marginal revenue product (MRP)—change in total revenue with the addition of one more unit of resource input for production.

marginal utility—the use a consumer gains from the addition of one more unit of a g/s.

market failure—the inability of the free market to provide public goods; over- or underallocation of g/s that have negative/positive externalities; used to justify government intervention.

Medicaid—entitlement program that finances medical costs for needy individuals.

Medicare—compulsory hospital insurance for the elderly, supplied by federal government through transfer payments of taxed wages.

microeconomics—portion of economics concerned with the individual elements that make up the economy: households, firms, government, and resource input prices.

monetarism—economic belief that the main cause of change in aggregate output and price level is movement in the money supply and the resultant interest rate.

monetary policy—policy basis on which the Federal Reserve influences interest rates through manipulation of the money supply to promote price stability, full employment, and productivity growth.

money—any article (paper note, metal coin) generally accepted as having value in exchange for a g/s.

money supply—defined, measured, and reported as M_1, M_2, M_3.

monopsony—a market structure in which there is only one buyer of a resource input or g/s.

MR = MC principle—law stating that to maximize profit and minimize loss, a firm will produce at the output level where the marginal revenue is equal to the marginal cost.

MRP = MRC formula—equation showing that to maximize profit and minimize loss, a firm will employ a resource input quantity when the marginal revenue product is equal to the marginal resource cost of the resource input.

multiplier—the effect that a change in one of the four components of aggregate expenditure has on GDP.

national (public) debt—money owed by the federal government to owners of government securities, equal to the total amount of money borrowed during all deficit spending.

natural monopoly—an industry in which the economy of scale is so large that one producer is the most efficient least-cost producer; usually regulated by government.

natural rate of unemployment—frictional and structural unemployment, the full employment rate, zero cyclical unemployment.

Neo-classical economics—school of economic thought holding that macroeconomic instability is a short-run event, and that the economy is stable at full employment in the long run because prices and wages automatically adjust for downturns in GDP, causing an eventual return to full employment, noninflationary output.

net export effect—any monetary or fiscal policy action is magnified (+ or −) by the effect that the change in U.S. dollar value (interest rates effect exchange rates) has on import and export prices.

Natural rate of unemployment—is a fluctuating rate determined by adding frictional to structural unemployment.

"nominal"—any economic measurement that is unadjusted for inflation.

nominal interest rate—the interest rate unadjusted for inflation.

normal good—a g/s the consumption of which increases as income increases (opposite of inferior g/s).

normal profit—where price equals average total cost, and cost includes the implicit cost of entrepreneurial value.

North American Free Trade Agreement (NAFTA)—1993 trade agreement between Canada, the United States, and Mexico, designed to reduce trade barriers over a 15-year period.

oligopoly—a market structure in which a few firms have a large market share and sell differentiated products. In oligopolies, firms tend to have large economies of scale, pricing is mutually dependent, and price wars can occur; there is a kinked-demand curve.

Organization of Petroleum Exporting Countries (OPEC)—a cartel that has control of about 60% of the world's oil and has at times effected severe price change by limiting production quotas.

partnership—an unincorporated firm with shared ownership.

PCE index—an inflation measurement indicator that includes current goods and services consumption, chain linked to their prior year prices.

perfectly elastic demand—infinite quantity demanded at a particular price; graphed as a straight horizontal line.

perfectly elastic supply—infinite quantity supplied at a particular price; graphed as a straight horizontal line.

perfectly inelastic demand—quantity demanded does not change in response to a change in price; graphed as a vertical straight line.

perfectly inelastic supply—quantity supplied does not change in response to a change in price; graphed as a horizontal straight line.

Phillips Curve (short-run)—a model that demonstrates the inverse relationship between unemployment (horizontal) and inflation (vertical axis).

Phillips Curve (long-run)—a model that demonstrates that after inflation expectations have been adjusted for, there is no trade off between inflation and unemployment, as it is vertical and equal to the NRU.

policy mix—recognition that fiscal and monetary policies are not independent and that in some circumstances are a necessary complement to each other.

price—the sum of money necessary to purchase a g/s.

Price = MC—in a purely competitive market model, the principle that a firm's demand is perfectly elastic and equal to price, so that a firm will maximize profit when price equals marginal cost if price is equal to or greater than ATC and minimize loss if price is greater than AVC.

price ceiling—a price set below equilibrium by government.

price elasticity of demand—percentage of change in quantity demanded divided by percentage of change in price; measures responsiveness to price changes.

price elasticity of supply—percentage of change in quantity supplied divided by percentage of change in price; measures responsiveness to price changes.

price fixing—illegal collusion between producers to set an above-equilibrium price.

price floor—a price set above equilibrium by government.

producer surplus—that portion of the supply curve that lies below equilibrium price and denotes producers that would bring the g/s to market at even lower prices.

progressive tax—a marginal tax rate system in which the percentage of tax increases as income increases and vice versa (such as U.S. federal income tax brackets).

proportional tax—a flat tax system in which the percentage of tax remains fixed as income changes.

public good—a g/s provided by government for which price does not exclude use and use is indivisible into individual components.

pure competition—market structure in which so many firms produce a very similar g/s that no firm has significant control over market price; a "price taker."

pure monopoly—market structure in which one firm is the sole producer of a distinct g/s and thus has significant control over market price; a "price maker."

quantity demanded—various amounts along a consumer demand curve showing the quantity consumers will buy at various prices.

quantity supplied—various amounts along a producer supply curve showing the quantity producers will sell at various prices.

"real"—an economic measurement (such as GDP or income) that has been adjusted for inflation.

recession—two consecutive business quarters of negative real GDP.

regressive tax—a set tax percentage the average rate of which decreases as the taxpayer's income increases, and vice versa; an example is sales tax.

required reserve ratio—a legally fixed percentage of a bank's reserves (demand deposits) that must be deposited with a Federal Reserve Bank.

Say's Law—a controversial generalization that the production of goods and services creates an equal demand for those g/s. Associated with economic policies under President Reagan.

shortage—difference between the quantity demanded of a g/s and the quantity supplied at a below-equilibrium price ($Q_d > Q_s$).

short run—the length of time during which a producer is unable to alter all the inputs of production.

shut-down point—point at which a firm will cease production because revenue would fall below average variable cost.

sole proprietorship—an unincorporated business owned by an individual.

specialization—concentration of resource(s) in the production of a g/s that results in increased efficiency of production.

spillover benefit—positive externality. Production or consumption results in benefits (such as education) not intended by the market participants.

spillover cost—negative externality. Production or consumption results in costs (such as pollution) not borne by the market participants.

stock—an ownership share in a company held by an investor.

structural unemployment—unemployment resulting from a mismatch of worker skill to demand or location.

subsidy—government financial support for which no direct payment is collected.

substitute—goods or services that are interchangeable. When the price of one increases, the demand for the other increases.

supply-side economics—macroeconomic perspective that emphasizes fiscal policies aimed at altering the state of the economy through I_g (short run) and the aggregate supply (long run).

surplus—difference between the quantity demanded of a g/s and the quantity supplied at an above-equilibrium price ($Q_d < Q_s$).

tariff—a tax on imports/exports.

tax—a required payment of money to government, for which the payer receives no direct g/s.

tight money policy—policy basis on which the Federal Reserve system acts to contract the money supply and increase interest rates, thereby slowing the economy.

trade deficit—amount by which a nation's imports exceed its exports.

trade-off—forgone alternative use of a resource in the production of a g/s.

trade surplus—amount by which a nation's exports exceed its imports.

variable cost—cost of inputs that fluctuates as a firm increases or decreases its output.

World Bank—organization that lends to developing nations to assist them in achieving economic growth.

World Trade Organization (WTO)—group established by the Uruguay Round of the GATT to assist in the promotion of trade and resolution of trade disputes.

ANSWER
SHEETS

INDEX

Index

REA'S
PROBLEM SOLVERS®

The PROBLEM SOLVERS® are comprehensive supplemental textbooks designed to save time in finding solutions to problems. Each PROBLEM SOLVER® is the first of its kind ever produced in its field. It is the product of a massive effort to illustrate almost any imaginable problem in exceptional depth, detail, and clarity. Each problem is worked out in detail with a step-by-step solution, and the problems are arranged in order of complexity from elementary to advanced. Each book is fully indexed for locating problems rapidly.

Accounting	Genetics
Advanced Calculus	Geometry
Algebra & Trigonometry	Linear Algebra
Automatic Control Systems/Robotics	Mechanics
Biology	Numerical Analysis
Business, Accounting & Finance	Operations Research
Calculus	Organic Chemistry
Chemistry	Physics
Differential Equations	Pre-Calculus
Economics	Probability
Electrical Machines	Psychology
Electric Circuits	Statistics
Electromagnetics	Technical Design Graphics
Electronics	Thermodynamics
Finite & Discrete Math	Topology
Fluid Mechanics/Dynamics	Transport Phenomena

*If you would like more information about any of these books,
complete the coupon below and return it to us or visit your local bookstore.*

Research & Education Association
61 Ethel Road W., Piscataway, NJ 08854
Phone: (732) 819-8880   **website: www.rea.com**

Please send me more information about your Problem Solver® books.

Name _____

Address _____

City _____ State _____ Zip _____
